Common Edible and Poisonous Mushrooms of the Northeast

**C. Leonard Fergus
and Charles Fergus**

STACKPOLE BOOKS

Published by
STACKPOLE BOOKS
An imprint of The Globe Pequot Publishing Group, Inc.
64 South Main Street
Essex, CT 06426
www.globepequot.com

Cover design by Wendy Reynolds
Cover photos by Charles Fergus

Library of Congress Cataloging-in-Publication Data

Fergus, Charles L.
    Common edible and poisonous mushrooms of the northeast /
C. Leonard Fergus and Charles Fergus.—1st ed.
        p. cm.
    Includes bibliographical references (p.).
    ISBN 0-8117-2641-X
        1. Mushrooms, Edible—Northeastern States—Identification.
    2. Mushrooms, Poisonous—Northeastern States—Identification.
    3. Mushrooms, Edible—Northeastern States—Pictorial works.
    4. Mushrooms, Poisonous—Northeastern States—Pictorial works.
    I. Fergus, Charles. II. Title

QK617 .F47 2003
579.6'0974—dc21
ISBN 978-0-8117-2641-2

The humblest fungus betrays a life akin to our own.
It is a successful poem in its kind.

Henry David Thoreau
October 10, 1858

Contents

Introduction

My father, C. Leonard Fergus, lived from 1917 to 1986. When he brought out this booklet on mushrooms in 1960, he was a professor of mycology and plant pathology (fungi and plant diseases) at Pennsylvania State University. The booklet, a basic guide for beginning mushroom hunters, was originally published by Penn State's College of Agriculture under the title *Some Common Edible and Poisonous Mushrooms of Pennsylvania*. The forty-three mushrooms described herein have a greater range than Pennsylvania, and this publication is pertinent for northeastern North America, roughly from the Mississippi River east and from Virginia north to southern Canada. Many of the species also occur in the Midwest and the South.

For years, different people have suggested that I republish my father's booklet, long out of print. I have a fair knowledge of mushrooms myself. When I was young, my father often took me along when he went collecting specimens to show to his students or to place in the university's Mycological Herbarium, of which he was the curator. I could recite the scientific names of many fungi before I knew my multiplication tables. Looking for mushrooms was a treasure hunt, with my father's approbation the reward when I spotted a colorful cap tucked away in the leaf mold or peeking up at the base of a log. Much later, as a science writer at Penn State, I took my father's advanced mycology course—the last time he taught it before he retired. We keyed out many specimens and also studied mushrooms under the microscope—their gills or spines or pores, their spore-bearing structures, and the spores themselves—which revealed another level of beauty in those mysterious, ephemeral fruits.

The mushrooms in this book are like old friends to me. I have dined on the edible ones and admired and photographed many others. Mushrooms are evanescent; they are the outward evidence of unseen organisms dwelling in trees and the earth, and they appear like spirits. It still thrills me to find a ring of Meadow Mushrooms newly sprung up in a pasture, a troop of King Boletes on the forest floor, the dazzling irruption of a Sulphur Shelf on an oak stump, or a Destroying Angel standing ominous in its cloak of white.

A word about taxonomy. As they are wont to do with all living things, scientists classify fungi: they place them in groups and give them names based on their physical characteristics. In a booklet of this scope, one need be concerned only with the categories *genus* and *species*. Take the dramatic, dangerous Destroying Angel as an example: it is assigned the scientific name *Amanita virosa*. This signifies that it belongs to genus *Amanita* (from the Greek *amanitai,* a fungus), a related group of numerous attractive fungi, many of them poisonous; and gives it its own identity as the type or species *A. virosa*, Latin *viros* for poisonous.

In updating my father's text, to keep pace with scientific advances in mushroom classification, I have changed the taxonomic names he used; alternate or former names are included in parentheses. For each species, I checked in current guides and made sure my father's original description was accurate. In some cases I added new findings or pertinent information that may have been left out of the original publication because of space constraints.

I was fortunate to locate the original negatives for the photographs illustrating the different mushrooms. The glass plate negatives were being stored in a sturdy oak cabinet at Penn State's Mont Alto campus near Chambersburg. (As of this writing, the negatives and mycological specimens are scheduled to be transferred to the U.S. Department of Agriculture, Beltsville, Maryland.) Lee O. Overholts, a professor in the botany department of Penn State, had taken the photographs mainly in the 1930s. I want to particularly thank Herb Cole and Eva Pell, Penn State faculty members and administrators, for making it possible for us to reuse those excellent images.

A mushroom, no matter its shape or color or size, is a fruiting body of an organism known as a *fungus* (plural, *fungi*). The fungi have an entire kingdom to themselves in the taxonomic system, separate from the plants. While resembling plants in their immobility, fungi lack the green pigment chlorophyll and obtain essential carbon compounds not by manufacturing them, as plants do through photosynthesis, but by gleaning them from living or dead matter. Fungi break down and consume plants: grasses, leaves, wood, fruit, and other plant parts. The fungi—which include molds, yeasts, smuts, and mildews—are key decomposers of vegetation, and without them, life on earth would be utterly different than we know it.

In the past, people thought mushrooms emerged spontaneously out of rotting matter or grew where lightning struck the ground. Not until the eighteenth century did humans discover that fungi exist as *hyphae*, strands of living tissue that spread through square yards or even acres of earth. We see their gossamer filaments when we turn over a clump of rotten leaves, dig in the upper layers of the soil, or break apart an old log. In the soil, fungal hyphae often infiltrate the fine outer rootlets of trees, helping the trees take in minerals and other nutrients by linking them to the vast network of fungal filaments. Some trees cannot survive without their mycorrhizal (*myco* for fungi, *rhizal* for root) partners. In return, the fungi receive carbon compounds that the trees make through photosynthesis. This symbiotic relationship explains why many fungi are found in forests.

Some mushrooms fruit in "fairy rings," so named because people once believed that fairies danced around the rings and sat on the mushrooms to rest. Fairy rings mark the outer edge of an underground fungus. The rings often show up in open areas such as fields and lawns, increasing in diameter each year as the fungal hyphae use up nutrients in the soil and expand outward. Some rings are hundreds of years old and cover several acres.

When the hyphae from two fungi of the same species meet, they may combine their genetic material and, when conditions are right, send forth mushrooms. Mushrooms are to fungi as apples are to apple trees. Because the underground or otherwise hidden fungus needs moisture to produce its fruit, mushrooms often appear two or three days after a soaking rain. Perhaps another reason that mushrooms arise during damp periods is that rain is often followed by dry, breezy conditions, perfect for the dissemination of mushroom spores.

Spores are analogous to the seeds in apples, except that spores are microscopic (most consist of a single cell) and are produced in mind-boggling numbers. Elio Schaechter, in his lively book *In the Company of Mushrooms: A Biologist's Tale,* writes: "A middle-sized mushroom with a four-inch cap may produce on the order of 20 billion spores over a period of four to six days, at a rate of some 100 million per hour." Depending on the shape and structure of the mushroom, its spores are ejected from between gills, trickle down through pores, waft away from branching structures, or come puffing out of bladders. Wind disperses the spores, sometimes carrying them for many miles. The spores land on the ground or on wood, where they form filaments that grow to become new fungi.

The color of a mushroom's spores is an important aid in identifying a fungus species. My father recommended placing a mushroom cap, minus its stem, on a combination of black and white paper, covering it with a jar or cup, and waiting an hour or so for a spore print to form: the print visible against either the white background or the black, depending on spore color. Other authorities suggest making spore prints on glass, then scraping the spores together with a knife blade to determine the color. Or one can make a spore print on transparent plastic, which can be held up against different-colored backgrounds to ascertain spore color.

Collecting mushrooms is a popular hobby. Although some fungi are edible, others are poisonous, and there are no hard and fast rules or tests by which a poisonous type can safely be discerned, other than by correctly identifying it. My father was fond of the saying "There are old mushroom hunters and bold mushroom hunters, but there are no old, bold mushroom hunters." Fortunately, most of the poisonous species are not fatal to people who ingest them: they bring on symptoms that resemble food poisoning, including nausea, cramps, vomiting, and diarrhea, lasting one or more days. Some mushrooms cause hallucinations. In general, the faster such symptoms show up, the less severe the ultimate outcome. Some mushrooms, however, deal death. Toward the end of this book, see "Destroying Angel," an essay I wrote some years ago, included here as a cautionary.

A friend of mine recently became enthusiastic about mushroom hunting. He equipped himself with several field guides and headed into the woods. Later he confided to me, "You really can't tell if something is a horse or an ass just from pictures in a book." He stressed the importance of collecting with a trustworthy tutor having close knowledge of the local fungi. I was lucky; my tutor was a professor of mycology. One can also get help from mycological societies and mushroom clubs (over a hundred in North America), and some schools and universities offer courses in mushroom identification.

To safely eat wild mushrooms, stick to easily identifiable ones that have no poisonous look-alikes. My father recommended what he called the "Foolproof Five": Shaggy Mane *(Coprinus comatus)*, Morels or Sponge Mushrooms *(Morchella* species), Sulphur Shelf or Chicken of the Woods *(Laetiporus sulphureus)*, Oyster Mushroom *(Pleurotus ostreatus)*, and Giant Puffball *(Calvatia gigantea)*.

The following precautions are in addition to those my father listed in his text:

- Thoroughly cook all mushrooms before eating.
- When trying a mushroom for the first time, eat only a small amount (remember, only eat one type of mushroom at a time). Save an uncooked specimen in the refrigerator for at least forty-eight hours; if symptoms develop, a mycologist can identify the mushroom, helpful to a doctor trying to treat any illness.
- Avoid feeding mushrooms to children, sick people, and the elderly, who are generally more susceptible to toxins than healthy adults.
- Do not pick mushrooms in contaminated places such as dumps, roadsides, industrial sites, and lawns and fields treated with pesticides. Some mushrooms concentrate environmental toxins.

You don't have to eat mushrooms to enjoy seeking and identifying them. Mushroom hunting is a great excuse to get out into the fields and forests, and learning about the lives of fungi opens up a new understanding of nature's cycles.

Charles Fergus
Port Matilda, PA

IMPORTANT NOTE

This book, although it describes and shows pictures of edible and poisonous mushrooms, should not be interpreted as advocating the eating of wild mushrooms. If a person does not know beyond a shadow of a doubt what sort of mushroom he or she has picked, *it should not be eaten.* Remember also that some people are allergic to mushrooms. Stackpole Books, its staff, and the author bear no liability for the use of information contained in this book.

Important Parts of Mushrooms

This book is intended as a basic guide for persons untrained in mycology who wish to identify the common mushrooms that seem to appear from nowhere each year in lawns, fields, and woods. In order to separate harmless and edible species from poisonous kinds, the observer must be able to recognize certain important parts of mushrooms. These parts—some with their scientific as well as their common names—are presented with the drawing below and in the following list:

Guide to Parts of Mushrooms

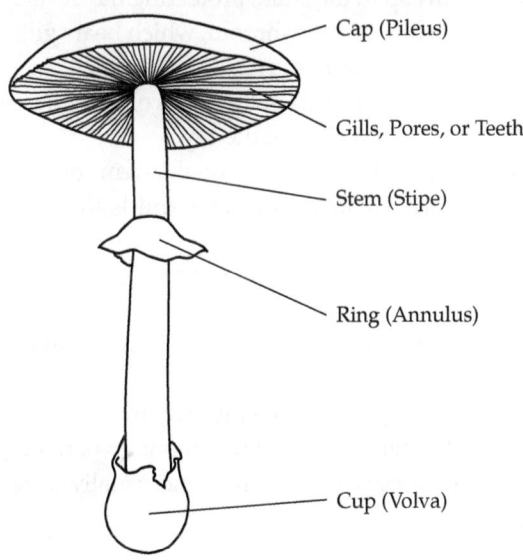

Cap (Pileus)

Gills, Pores, or Teeth

Stem (Stipe)

Ring (Annulus)

Cup (Volva)

Annulus. The remnants of the partial veil, useful in the identification of certain mushrooms. See *ring.*

Bulb. A swelling at the base of the stem.

Cap. The expanded and often flattened part, usually at the top of a mushroom's stem. The underside of the cap bears the spore-dispensing gills, pores, or teeth. See *pileus.*

Convex. Rounded or regularly elevated toward the center; used in describing the caps of certain mushrooms.

Cup. The scales or sheath seen at the base of the stem in some mushrooms. The cup is the remnant of the universal veil that completely encloses the developing mushroom at first, but is ultimately broken and left at the base, usually partly underground. See *universal veil* and *volva.*

Flesh. The inner substance of the stem or cap, exclusive of the external layer and of gills, pores, or teeth.

Gills. Leaflike plates on the undersurface of the cap. See also *pores, teeth,* and *tubes.*

Lateral. Attached to one side of the cap; used in describing the stems of some mushrooms.

Partial veil. A membrane that extends from the unopened margin of a mushroom cap to the stalk, protecting the developing gills.

Pileus. The cap portion of a mushroom, which bears gills, pores, or teeth on the lower side. See *cap.*

Pores. The openings at the ends of the tubes of certain mushrooms, visible on the undersurface of the cap.

Ring. The remnants of the partial veil on the stems of certain mushrooms. It usually encircles the stem and is therefore called a ring. See *annulus.*

Scale. A more or less raised portion of the outer, skinlike layer of the cap.

Spores. Tiny reproductive bodies of mushrooms, akin to the seeds of plants.

Stem. Stalk supporting the cap of a mushroom.

Stuffed. Said of the stem on some mushrooms, when the interior is filled with a material different from and usually softer than the outer part.

Teeth. Thornlike or spinelike structures on the undersurface of the caps or branches of certain mushrooms.

Tubes. Tubular or pipelike structures arranged vertically in the caps of certain mushrooms. Seen only when the cap is cut through.

Universal veil. A membrane surrounding the young developing mushroom in some species. See *cup* and *volva*.

Umbo. A raised knob in the middle of a mushroom's cap.

Volva. The cuplike structure surrounding the bases of some mushrooms, and a key identification mark for several poisonous species. See *cup*.

Some Common Edible and Poisonous Mushrooms of the Northeast

C. Leonard Fergus

Many species of fungi grow wild in eastern North America. With their sudden and bizarre appearance, rapid growth, striking colors, and possible use as food, mushrooms interest people of diverse ages and backgrounds. Mushrooms also are excellent objects for nature study and matchless photographic subjects.

As sources of food, wild mushrooms may be divided into those known to be dangerously poisonous, slightly poisonous, suspected, disagreeable in taste, edible but of mediocre quality, and of excellent flavor. The possibility of individual variable allergic reactions to mushrooms, just as to eggs and strawberries, must also be considered.

In this publication an attempt is made to describe, by means of text and photographs, some of the common edible mushrooms found in this region. Poisonous species are included so that collectors may know when and where to expect to find them and thus avoid them.

According to estimates, several thousand kinds of fungi appear in the Northeast. It is beyond the scope of this publication to consider them all. Obviously, the collector will encounter many mushrooms not included, since only forty-three are described. However, the ones included are quite common and will be found more frequently than the ratio would indicate.

The mushrooms described herein have been selected for various reasons. First, each possesses characteristics so distinctive that the average person may quickly learn to know them. Second, of the edible mushrooms listed, only those are included that have no suspicious history. Third, they are quite common, having been collected many times, in many places, year after year.

No rules are known by which an inexperienced person can distinguish poisonous from edible mushrooms. To be safe, a collector must be able to recognize edible species just as he or she recognizes a violet or a rose. The edibility of many of our wild mushrooms still is not known. One cannot tell by looking at any plant whether it is poisonous or not. Keep in mind that the only way to determine if a plant is poisonous is for someone to have been poisoned by it after eating it, and the same is true for mushrooms.

The following important precautions should be rigidly observed:

- Do not eat any mushroom that you cannot definitely identify and that has not been recorded as edible.
- Do not eat any mushroom just because it is not recognizable as of a poisonous species.
- Never eat a mushroom that is beginning to discolor or deteriorate, or that has been partially devoured or invaded by insects.
- Be sure to dig up the entire mushroom so that all underground parts will be collected. Never eat a mushroom that has both a cup (volva) at the base of the stem and a ring (annulus) around the upper part of the stem.
- Do not mix the mushrooms that you find. Sort them carefully, and keep each collection separate. Use coffee cans, paper bags, or waxed paper parcels; plastic bags trap moisture, leading to deterioration.
- Be extremely careful in the identification of any mushroom that has a white spore print or is in the early stage of development (button stage). At this time, certain important identifying characteristics will not yet be discernible. If in doubt about the identity of a specimen and the fruiting body is a gilled mushroom, a spore print should be made unless

positive determination of the color of the expelled spores en masse is possible from the ground or debris at the time of collection. Spores are very small and are visible to the naked eye only when massed in large numbers. To make a spore print, always select a mature specimen. Cut the stem off flush with the gills and lay the cap, gills down, partly on white paper and partly on black paper. Cover this arrangement with a jar or cup so that air currents will not disrupt the spores and the mushroom will not dry out too rapidly. A spore print should become evident in one to two hours. You can determine the spore color as white, rosy or pink, yellow- to rusty-brown, dark brown or purple-brown, or black. Spore prints are beautiful. They may be used for decoration if sprayed with a fixative, such as a clear lacquer available at an arts and crafts store.

- If necessary, or if it is discovered that a poisonous fungus has been eaten, induce vomiting immediately and call your doctor or Poison Control Center.

AIDS IN IDENTIFICATION

A key in mycology is simply a specialized shortcut to positive identification. In the identification of mushrooms, one choice after another is eliminated until there is left but a single one to which the mushroom at hand can be assigned. The use of a key demands continual choosing: either the mushroom at hand does or does not exhibit a certain characteristic. When using a key, great care must be taken in making the various choices.

Let us select *Pleurotus ostreatus,* the Oyster Mushroom, as an example and attempt to key it down, using the key presented on pages 15–16. Start with choice 1 in the key. The specimen is a mushroom with gills on the underside of the cap; hence, move to choice 2. Does it have a ring on the stem or not? (See the drawing on page 7 for an illustration of a ring.) It does not; move to choice 5. The gills or cap do not exude a milky juice when broken, so move to choice 6. Is the spore print white or black? Since it is white, go to choice 8. The gills are sharp-edged; therefore, move to choice 9. The stem is lateral: thus, the mushroom is classified in the genus *Pleurotus* or the very closely related genus *Hypsizygus*. Turn to the pages on which those mushrooms are described and compare your specimens with the text descriptions and photographs. If they agree, you know you have collected *Pleurotus ostreatus*. If the description of that species does not coincide closely with your specimen, or if you cannot find a name in the key of a mushroom that agrees with your find, you probably have collected a mushroom not included in this publication. You should discard such a collection unless you have available more complete and detailed mushroom books.

The mushrooms are described in the text in the same order as they are presented in the key.

Each description of a mushroom includes color, size, presence or absence of a ring (annulus) and a cup (volva), presence of gills or pores or teeth, locations or habitats where the species commonly occurs, substratum on which it usually grows (soil, rotting wood, etc.), season in which it usually appears, and other items of interest. Many mushrooms develop only in certain months, whereas others appear throughout the growing season. Weather influences the time when mushrooms fruit. In general, the broadest range of species and the greatest number of mushrooms emerge from late summer into early or mid-fall.

Joining a mushroom club is one of the best ways to learn how to identify wild mushrooms. Two particular organizations are of great help to amateur mushroom collectors and can offer information about local mushroom clubs. They are the North American Mycological Association (www.namyco.org), at 6615 Tudor Court, Gladstone, Oregon 97027-1032, and the Northeast Mycological Federation (www.nemf.org), at 141 River Road, Millington, New Jersey 07946-1303.

It's also a good idea to find the phone number of the local Poison Control Center and have it handy before you need it. The emergency phone number of the American Association of Poison Control Centers is 1-800-222-1222.

KEY TO SOME COMMON
EDIBLE AND POISONOUS MUSHROOMS

1. Mushrooms with gills on underside of cap

  2. Mushrooms with ring on the stem

    3. Mushrooms with volva at base of stem . . . .*Amanita*

    3. Mushrooms without volva

      4. Purple-brown spore print . . . .*Agaricus, Psathyrella,*
Hypholoma

      4. White or green spore print . . . .*Armillaria, Macrolepiota,*
Chlorophyllum, Lepiota

  2. Mushrooms without ring

    5. Gills or cap exuding a milky juice if broken . . . .*Lactarius*

    5. Without milky juice

      6. Spore print black

        7. Gills and cap dissolve at maturity
into black ink . . . .*Coprinus*

        7. Gills dark-spotted and do not
dissolve into ink . . . .*Panaeolus*

      6. Spore print white

        8. Gills blunt and thick on edge and
usually united in a network . . . .*Cantharellus*

        8. Gills sharp-edged

          9. Stem lateral . . . .*Pleurotus, Hypsizygus*

          9. Stem central

            10. Gills running down the stem . . . .*Omphalotus*

            10. Gills not running down the stem

              11. Edge of gills like saw-teeth . . . .*Lentinus*

              11. Edge of gills not saw-toothed

                12. Stem tough-brittle, breaking
with a snap . . . .*Oudesmansiella,*
Flammulina

                12. Stem fleshy-fibrous, not
breaking with a snap . . . .*Lepista*

1. Mushrooms without gills

   13. Mushrooms with many small pores on the underside
of the cap

      14. Stem central and unbranched . . . .*Boletus, Leccinum,
Suillus, Strobilomyces*

      14. Stem absent or lateral or branched multiple times . . . . . .*Fistulina,
Grifola, Laetiporus*

   13. Mushrooms without pores

      15. Fungi with teeth or spines on the pileus . . . .*Hericium, Hydnum*

      15. Fungi without teeth or spines

         16. Mushroom coral-shaped or club-shaped or
funnel-shaped

            17. Fungus looks like coral, consisting of
many small, upright branches . . . .*Clavaria, Ramaria*

            17. Fungus club-shaped or funnel-shaped . . . .*Craterellus,
Cantharellus*

         16. Mushroom looks like a sponge or saddle or ball

            18. Fungus looks like a sponge or saddle . . . .*Morchella,
Gyromitra*

            18. Fungus looks like a ball . . . .*Calvatia*

Gilled Fungi

Amanita species. All amanita mushrooms should be avoided, as many of the most deadly poisonous fungi belong to this genus. The following characteristics distinguish them: a white spore print; a ring or annulus on the stem; and a cup or volva at the base of the stem. The ring on the stem is usually easy to recognize; however, sometimes it is lost over time or in the expansion of the mushroom. Generally more than one specimen, each of different ages, are collected, and the younger ones should show the ring. The volva may be cuplike and membranous, in which case it is easily recognized. However, no distinct cup is formed in some species, as the volva breaks up into scales or crumbling particles. In some species, the volva is united with the base of the stem, giving it a bulbous appearance often detectable as concentric rings of tissue. The greatest danger is that the collector fails to dig up the complete specimen, so that the volva, much of which is below the ground, is left behind. Remember, never collect a specimen by just snapping it off or breaking it free—rather, dig it out carefully, using a knife or trowel, to be sure to get all the parts.

Amanita muscaria, the Fly Amanita or Fly Agaric (Poisonous). Fruits in summer and fall. Cap 3 to 8 inches broad, slightly slimy when young, bright yellow, sometimes with an orange-red center. The volva is seen as prominent scales encircling the bulbous base of the stem. Occurs in groups, sometimes in fairy rings in open woods (deciduous or coniferous) and in brushy pastures.

The common name comes from the practice of using the flesh, mixed with milk, to stupefy flies so they can be swatted more easily. Across the Northern Hemisphere, *Amanita muscaria* is quite

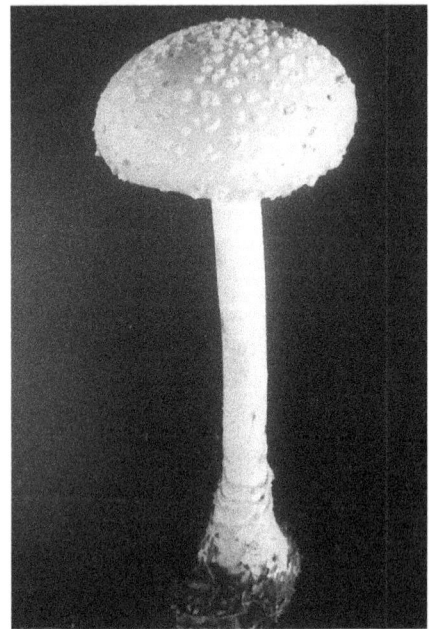

Amanita muscaria,
the Fly Amanita

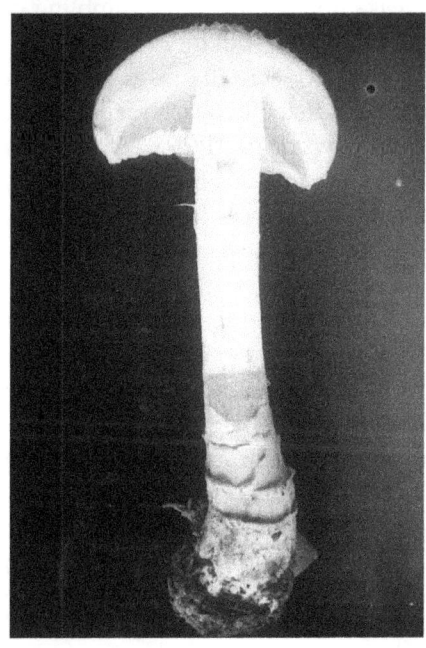

Amanita muscaria

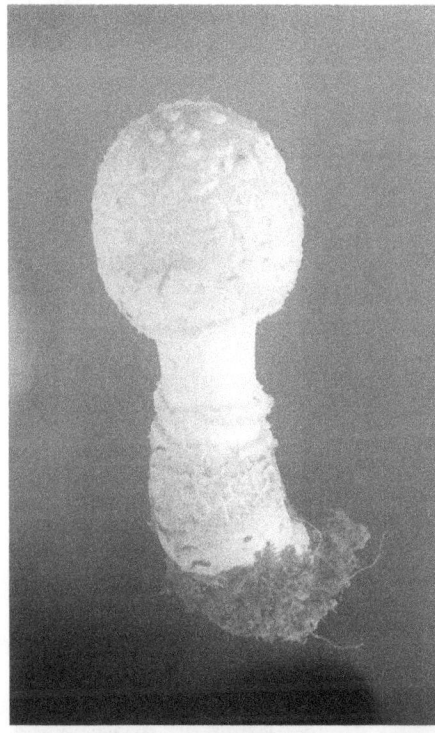

Immature stage of
Amanita muscaria

variable in the intensity of its red-orange-yellow cap coloration. The mushroom contains two kinds of toxins. One kind causes the heart to slow, the blood vessels to dilate, and the pupils to contract. The second kind is a hallucinogen acting on the central nervous system. Humans have been fatally poisoned by this mushroom. Anthropologists believe ancient peoples consumed the Fly Agaric as part of religious rituals.

Amanita virosa, the Destroying Angel (Poisonous). Summer and fall. Cap 2 to 4 inches broad, convex to flat, and smooth, without warts. The entire mushroom is pure white. The veil hangs like a dinner napkin around the stem, although sometimes it is torn or mostly falls off. The stem can be 6 inches or even longer and is enclosed at its base in a saclike volva, or cup. This common mush-

Amanita bisporigera,
all three photos

room is as beautiful and deadly as its name implies. See "Destroying Angel," page 77, for more information and a photograph.

Amanita bisporigera (Poisonous). Summer and fall. Closely related to *Amanita virosa* and similar in appearance, although often slightly smaller and with a more slender stalk. The main difference is that the basidia (microscopic spore-bearing structures in the gills) bear two spores in *Amanita bisporigera*, rather than four spores, as in *Amanita virosa*.

Amanita cothurnata (Poisonous). Summer and fall. The nearly white cap is flecked with small, wartlike patches, remnants of the universal veil that enclosed the developing mushroom. *Amanita cothurnata* is closely related to the Gem-Studded Amanita,

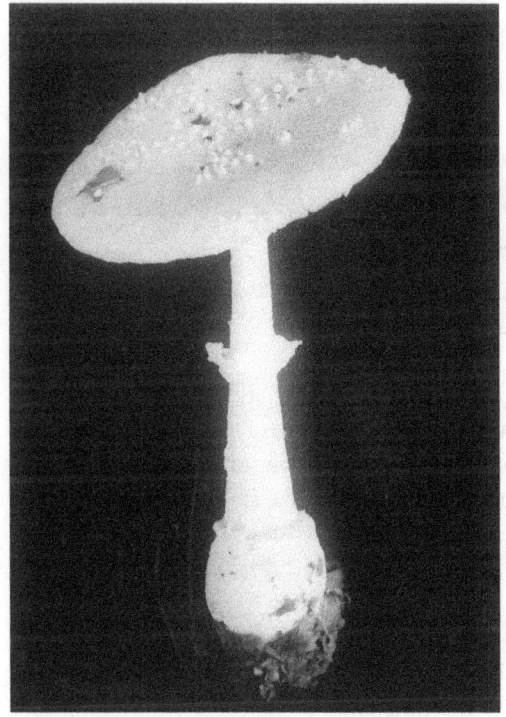

Amanita cothurnata

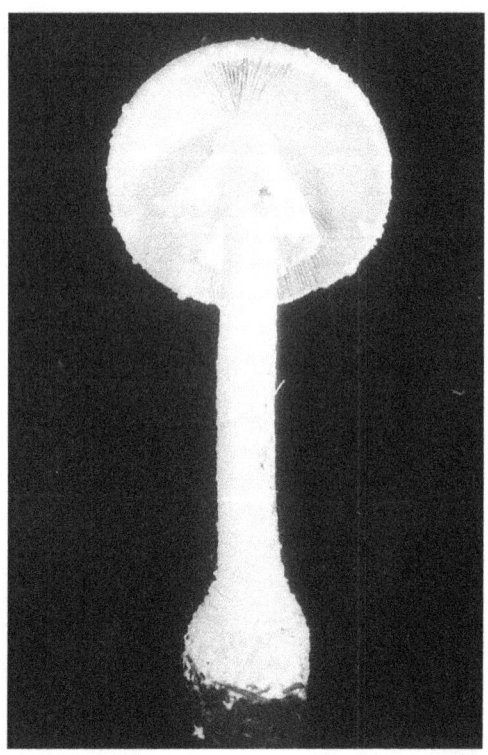

Amanita cokeri

Amanita gemmata, whose dull yellow cap is also decorated with white volval remnants.

Amanita cokeri (Poisonous). Summer and fall. The cap is 2 to 6 inches broad, ivory white, and topped with brownish warts. The volva sticks to the bulbous base and fragments into irregular patches. The prominent veil hangs skirtlike from the upper part of the stem. This mushroom is often found in the mid-Atlantic and the southern states. It is sometimes called *Amanita solitaria.*

Agaricus campestris, the Meadow Mushroom or Field Mushroom (Edible). Fruits in spring, during damp periods in summer, and in fall. Cap 1½ to 4 inches broad, at first convex, then almost flat when expanded, smooth, white or cream-colored, flesh firm and white; stem 2 to 3 inches long, ½ to ¾ inch thick, solid, white, smooth, with an annulus or ring at or near the middle but usually torn; gills pink or flesh-colored, protected by a delicate membrane (the annulus) when young, finally chocolate to blackish brown when the annulus detaches from the cap and becomes the ring. Spore print dark brown to purple-brown. Occurs as scattered small groups, sometimes in fairy rings, on open grassy land such as lawns, golf courses, park areas, cemeteries. The pink to blackish brown color of the gills and the distinct ring on the stem help to distinguish this from other mushrooms. The Meadow Mushroom ranges across North America. Several other *Agaricus* species, with similar gill color and ring, also are edible. Most of the mushrooms sold in grocery stores are in this genus.

Agaricus campestris, the Meadow Mushroom

Agaricus campestris

Psathyrella candolleana *(Hypholoma incertum)* (Edible). Fruits mainly in summer. Cap 1 to 3 inches across, rather thin, bell-shaped when young but umbrella-shaped later, and finally flat or level, appearing water-soaked, pale honey-yellow, then buff to white as the cap dries out, sometimes with a darker yellow center; stem 1½ to 3 inches long, ⅛ to ¼ inch thick, white, hollow, with a tendency to split lengthwise; veil (annulus) seen as soft, white fragments that cling to the edge of the cap or as a ring on the stem; gills at first white, then pale lilac, and finally purple-brown. Spore print dark brown to purple-brown. Usually occurs in large clusters in lawns, gardens, pastures, stumps, and occasionally associated with living deciduous trees; sometimes it fruits on or near rotting wood. Although edible, this smallish mushroom does not have much flesh.

Hypholoma sublateritium *(Naematoloma sublateritium),* the Brick Cap or Brick Top (Edible). Late summer and fall, often very late in autumn after most other fungi have quit fruiting. Cap dark brick red, sometimes tawny, margin of lighter color, convex at first, later nearly flat, smooth, sometimes with fine silky fibers, fleshy, 1 to 4 inches across; gills crowded, whitish, becoming olive, finally deep purple-brown; stem solid, upper part light, base same color as cap, sometimes curved, 3 to 6 inches long and ¼ to ½ inch thick. Spore print dark purple-brown (almost black). Occurs in dense clumps with numerous stems arising from the same place, on decaying logs, stumps, and tree roots, and on the ground near them.

The Brick Cap has a mild to somewhat bitter taste. The similar but less common Sulphur Tuft, *Hypholoma fasciculare*, is a yellow mushroom yielding a purple-brown spore print; it grows on logs and stumps. The Sulphur Tuft is very bitter. Poisonous, it causes nausea, vomiting, and abdominal pain.

Psathyrella candolleana

Hypholoma sublateritium,
the Brick Cap,
(above and below)

Armillaria mellea (*Armillariella mellea*), the Honey Mushroom or Oak Fungus (Edible). Late summer and fall, especially September and later if abundant rains occur. Cap 1 to 6 inches across, rather thin, at first hemispheric but finally flat, usually covered with numerous dark, hairy scales, especially in the center (however, scales may be lacking), pale yellow or reddish brown, slightly slimy when young; stem 1 to 6 inches long and ¼ to ¾ inch thick, base slightly hairy, pallid or brownish, stuffed at first but hollow when old; gills white, running slightly down the stem, when young covered by a veil that ruptures to leave a ring high up on the stem. Spore print white. Usually occurs as clusters on the ground, probably coming from buried roots, on stumps, and on wood of a great variety of trees but especially oaks. The greenish light known as foxfire comes from filaments of this fungus that have invaded stumps, downed limbs, and other woody debris.

The Honey Mushroom is quite variable in appearance. The best identifiers are its honey color, ring, scales, white spores, and habit

Armillaria mellea, the Honey Mushroom

Armillaria mellea

of growing on wood. The mushroom has an acrid taste that is lost when parboiled before final cooking. An important forest parasite, *Armillaria mellea* kills many trees. The fungus spreads by means of long black strands, or rhizomorphs, visible beneath the bark of infected trees; the disease is called shoestring root rot. *Armillaria mellea* can also survive as a typical fungal saprophyte, consuming dead organic matter.

The poisonous Jack-o'-Lantern Mushroom, *Omphalotus olearius,* which also grows from stumps and yields a white spore print, is orange in color. The Deadly Galerina, *Galerina autumnalis* (not covered in this book), also grows on wood in autumn; it is smaller, lacks hairs on the cap surface, and produces a rust-brown spore print.

Macrolepiota procera *(Lepiota procera),* the Parasol Mushroom (Edible). Summer and fall. Cap 3 to 6 inches across, ovate then expanded and flat, with a distinct smooth brown conical knob, or umbo. The cap is covered with a reddish to brownish skin that breaks up into brown scales showing the white inner flesh; the scales are part of the cap and are not remnants of the volva, as in *Amanita* species. Stem 5 to 12 inches long and slender, about ½ inch thick, thinner upward from a bulbous base, generally scaly or spotted; cap free from stem, and if removed a distinct socket remains in the cap; a very large, thick ring or annulus is present at maturity, which often can be moved up and down the stem like a bracelet. The spore print is white. Occurs singly or in scattered groups in lawns, meadows, pastures, open woods, and along roadsides.

Many foragers consider the Parasol Mushroom among the best-tasting of all edible mushrooms, but caution must be taken in identifying it. The similar *Chlorophyllum molybdites (Lepiota molybdites)* is a poisonous species that causes gastrointestinal upsets; it should

Macrolepiota procera,
the Parasol Mushroom

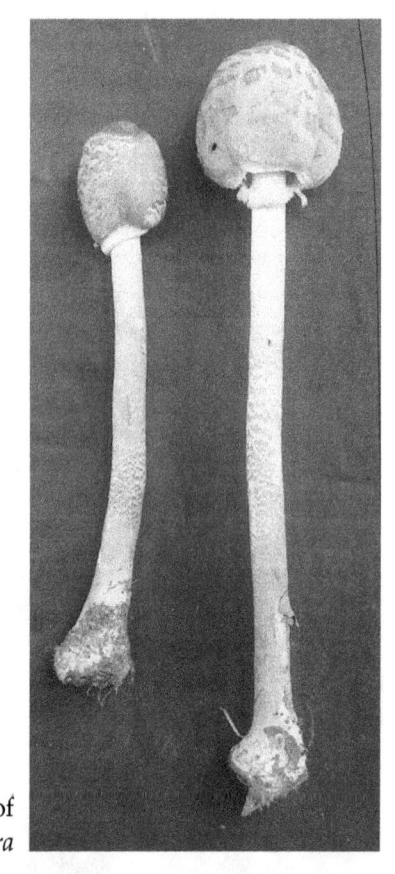

Immature stages of
Macrolepiota procera

not be mistaken for the Parasol Mushroom because mature *Chlorophyllum molybdites* have green gills, producing a green spore print, and the stem tends to be thicker and more club-shaped. Also, a rare related species, *Lepiota josserandii,* is reported to contain deadly amanitin toxins, the compounds that make some *Amanita* mushrooms so dangerous. *For this reason, many authorities recommend that none of the parasol-type mushrooms be eaten.*

Lactarius deliciosus, the Delicious Lactarius or Orange-Latex Milky (Edible). Late summer and fall. Cap 2 to 5 inches across, at first convex, later becoming shaped like a funnel, smooth, deep orange, fading to grayish yellow when old, the colors generally zoned, margin at first rolled in, then unfolding, flesh soft; cap, gills, and stems exude an orange milk, especially where wounded; stem 1 to 3 inches long and up to 1 inch thick, very squatty in appearance, stuffed or hollow. Spore print white. Occurs singly or in clusters of several individuals in mossy places and on the ground under conifers, especially pines. This species is highly prized as food and can be distinguished even by the beginner because of its orange color, concentric zones or rings of light and dark orange on the cap (these may be faint or not present), squat fat appearance, and orange

Lactarius deliciosus, the Delicious Lactarius

milk. The cap turns green if bruised and as it ages. Mycologists recognize several varieties of this common, widespread mushroom.

Lactarius indigo, the Blue Lactarius or Indigo Milky (Edible). Summer and fall. Cap 2 to 5 inches across, at first centrally depressed, later almost funnel-shaped, indigo blue or paler, fading when dry, with a silver-gray luster, smooth but with zones; stem 1 to 2 inches long and ¼ to 1 inch thick, smooth, stuffed or hollow, same color as cap; milk from cap, gills, and stem is abundant and dark blue. Flesh stains green when bruised. Spore print white, cream, or yellow. Comes up singly or in clusters on the ground in oak, maple, and pine woods, often after heavy rains. This species is

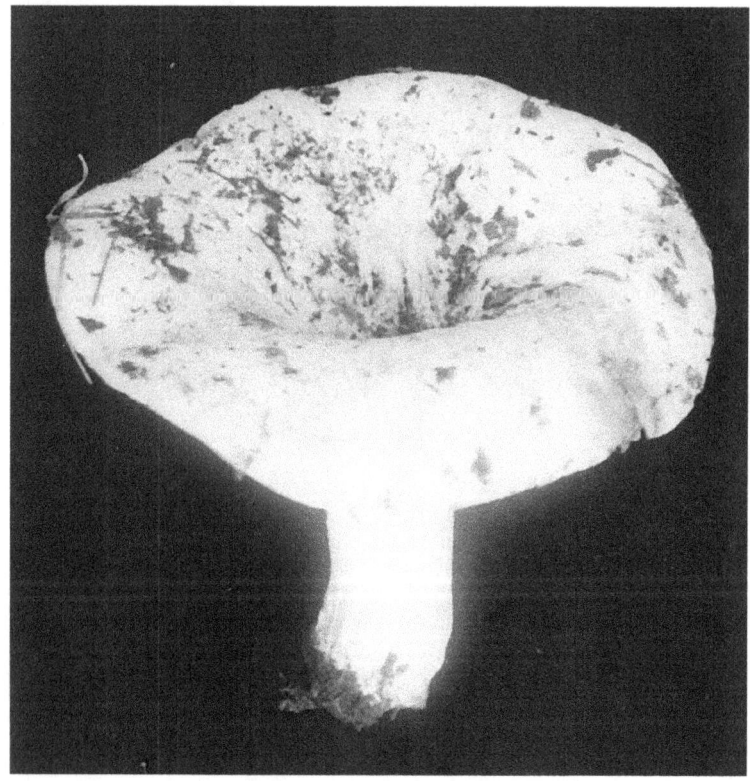

Lactarius indigo, the Blue Lactarius

unique in the striking blue color of its cap and milk, and its stout appearance. It is common in the South, less so in the North.

Coprinus atramentarius, the Inky Cap or Tippler's Bane (Edible). Summer and fall. Cap 1 to 3 inches across, conical, then becoming bell-shaped, with a grayish bloom that readily comes off, exposing the brown surface underneath; stem 2 to 4 inches long, hollow, smooth in the upper part but with scales below. At maturity, the gills dissolve into a thick, black fluid, with the spores carried away by insects or water rather than wind. Spore print black. Comes up in clusters, usually in rich soils such as in gardens, or in woods. All *Coprinus* species are short-lived mushrooms that must be prepared and eaten soon after picking: cooking disables the enzymes that otherwise break down their tissues.

Do not drink alcohol when eating *Coprinus atramentarius* or within three days of ingestion, or flushed skin, heart palpitations, nausea, and diarrhea may result. In the past, people boiled the caps of *Coprinus* mushrooms to make ink.

Coprinus comatus, the Shaggy Mane (Edible). Sometimes emerges in spring but appears more frequently in summer and fall. Easily distinguished from other fungi because the cap does not open wide to a horizontal position. Cap 2 to 3 inches long, expanding to about 5 inches in length, egg- to bell-shaped, whitish sometimes with pinkish shades, with many yellowish or reddish brown scales; stem 3 to 7 inches long, white, pointed at the base, hollow and smooth to silky; movable ring on stem. Spore print black. As the Shaggy Mane ages, it quickly breaks down into an inky mass, with dissolution, or deliquescence, starting on the hanging rim of the cap and progressing upward; this process continues even if the mushroom is refrigerated. *Coprinus comatus* grows singly or in clusters, rarely in fairy rings, on bare ground or in grass, in rich earth along roadsides, in pastures, lawns, gardens, and waste dumping grounds. Mushroom hunters often cook this flavorful mushroom with scrambled eggs; it is also excellent in soups, sauces, and gravies. In Britain, *Coprinus comatus* is dubbed the Lawyer's Wig.

Early stage of
Coprinus atramentarius

Coprinus atramentarius, the Inky Cap

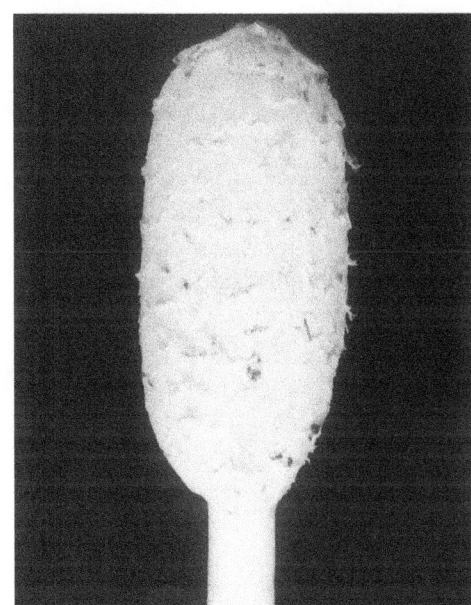

Coprinus comatus,
the Shaggy Mane

An aging
Coprinus comatus

Coprinus micaceus, the Mica Cap or Glistening Coprinus (Edible). Spring to fall. Cap 1 to 2 inches across, domelike or bell-shaped, the margin furrowed or striated, tawny-yellow to reddish brown, glistening with shiny particles that gradually rub off or are rinsed away by rain. Stem 1 to 3 inches long, slender, hollow, fragile. Spore print black. Occurs in dense clumps around bases of living trees or stumps, on lawns, and along sidewalks and streets. The young specimens are edible before their gills blacken and dissolve. Although small, this mushroom usually fruits in good quantities.

Panaeolus retirugis (Poisonous). Late spring and summer. Cap ½ to 1½ inches across; cone-shaped when young, later convex; dark gray, tan, or pale yellow-gray; smooth at the center but with other parts becoming cracked, wrinkled, or ridged. Stem 2 to 5 inches long, pale gray, darker at the base, hollow, fragile; gills at first white, then mottled dark gray or black. Spore print black. Usually occurs singly or in small groups, on manure heaps and in lawns and fields. This mushroom contains compounds causing sickness and hallucinations.

Cantharellus cibarius, the Golden Chanterelle (Edible). Summer and fall. Cap 1 to 4 inches across, dry, firm, fleshy, convex then expanded, sometimes funnel-shaped, bright yellow to orange-yellow, margin often wavy or irregular, curved, or upraised, flesh white or light yellowish; stem yellow, 1½ to 3 inches long, thick, firm, solid, smooth, usually tapering downward; gills thick-edged, forked or united in a network, also running down the stem, pale yellow. Spore print pale yellow. Occurs singly and in groups on the ground in deciduous and coniferous woods. Some sources cite an apricotlike aroma and a mild to somewhat peppery taste. Less common is the Red Chanterelle, *Cantharellus cinnabarinus,* also a choice edible. Be certain not to mistake the Chanterelles for the poisonous Jack-o'-Lantern, *Omphalotus olearius,* which is orange and can be somewhat similar in appearance.

Pleurotus ostreatus, the Oyster Mushroom (Edible). Late spring, summer, and fall, and occasionally during winter thaws.

Coprinus micaceus,
the Mica Cap

Panaeolus retirugis

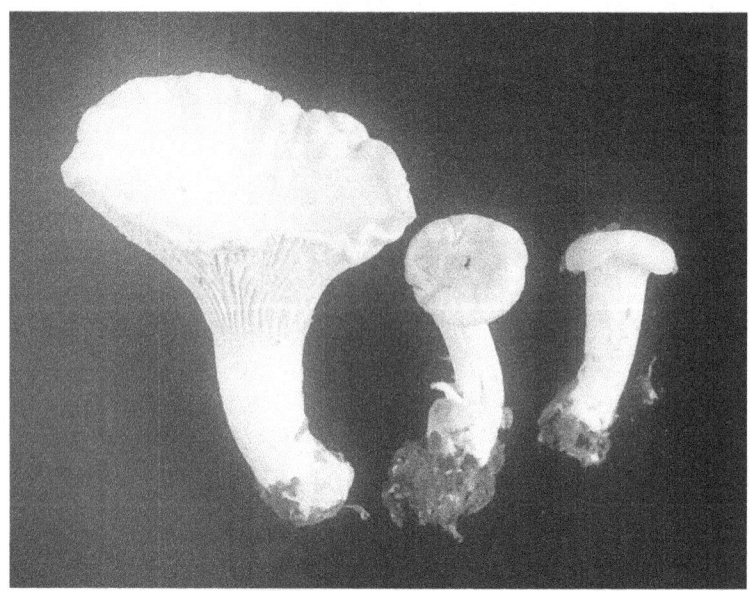

Cantharellus cibarius, the Golden Chanterelle

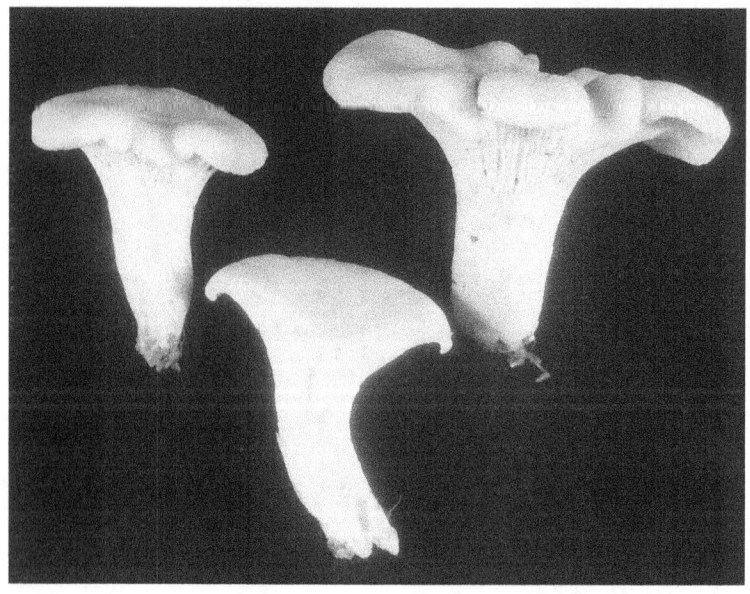

Cantharellus cibarius

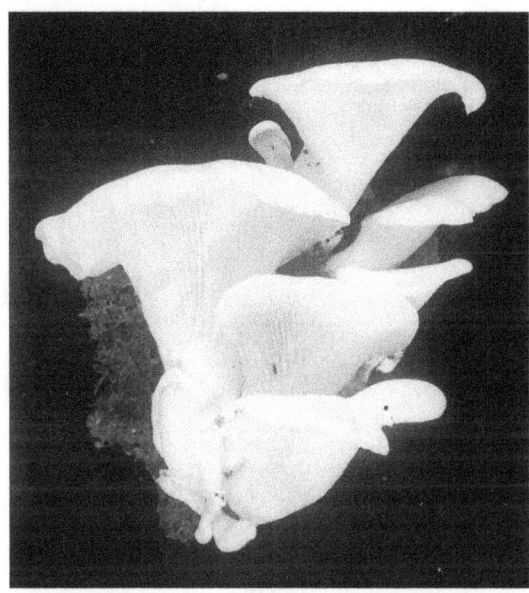

Pleurotus ostreatus, the Oyster Mushroom

Cap 2 to 5 inches across, convex, soft, whitish, grayish, or brownish, looking somewhat like a scallop shell, the flesh thick and white. Usually several caps shelve out one above the other. A stem may or may not be present; if so, it is short, 1 to 2 inches long, and lateral, sometimes hairy at the base. The gills are white, broad and running down onto the stem, and branching or fusing. Spore print white to buff or pale lilac. Occurs on decaying wood, stumps, and dead or dying trees, including elm, oak, beech, birch, maple, aspen, and willow; a single fungus may fruit several times in a given year. The lateral stem and growth from trees help to distinguish this species, for which there are no toxic look-alikes. Several species of beetles lay their eggs in the gills of the Oyster Mushroom; the resulting larvae ruin the mushroom by chewing holes and tunnels through the flesh when feeding.

Pleurotus sapidus (Edible). Similar to the Oyster Mushroom, *Pleurotus ostreatus,* except that it produces a grayish lilac spore print. This mushroom, which also sprouts from wood, often has a short, off-center stalk.

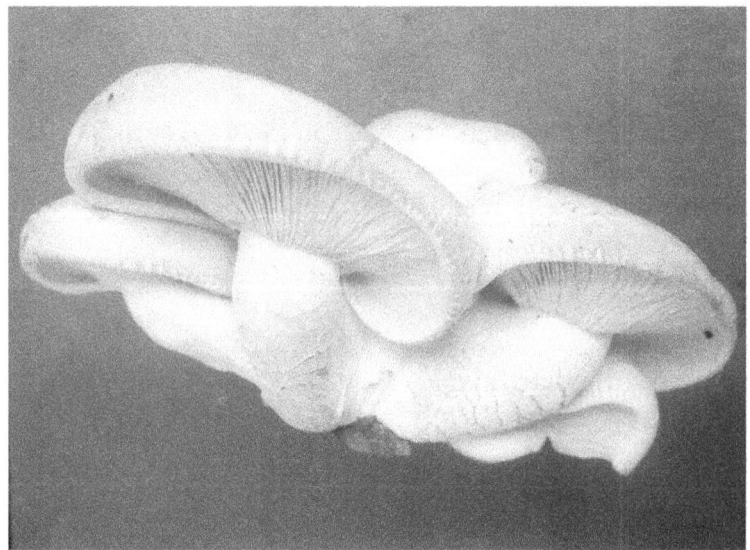

Hypsizygus tessulatus, the Elm Pleurotus

Hypsizygus tessulatus *(Pleurotus ulmarius)*, the Elm Pleurotus (Edible). Fall. Cap convex or nearly flat, white to creamy, sometimes tinged brownish or yellowish in the center, 3 to 6 inches across; flesh white, firm, thick; stem attached to the side of the cap, white, smooth or rarely hairy at the base, 2 to 4 inches long, ½ to ¾ inch thick. Spore print white to buff. Occurs in clusters or singly from wounds or stumps of cut branches on elm, maple, and other hardwoods. The flesh is tough and must be cooked thoroughly.

Omphalotus olearius *(Clitocybe illudens, Omphalotus illudens),* the Jack-o'-Lantern or False Chanterelle (Poisonous). Late summer and fall. Cap bright yellow or orange-yellow, 2 to 6 inches across, convex or flat, sometimes shallow funnel-shaped, often with a small conical knob (umbo) in the center, and sometimes with a strong, unpleasantly sweet odor; stem 2 to 7 inches long and ¼ to ¾ inch thick, uniformly thick except near the base, where it may taper to a point, pale yellow, solid, very fibrous and usually curved; gills running down the stem. Spore print creamy white to pale yellow. Usually occurs as dense clumps in woods and open places, especially on stumps and buried roots of oaks. The stems of five to twenty mushrooms may be fused into a common base. Can be distinguished from all other mushrooms by its color, like that of a ripe pumpkin, and its growth from a woody substrate.

The gills of the Jack-o'-Lantern bioluminesce, glowing greenish yellow in the dark. Take a specimen into a darkened room and wait three to four minutes for your eyes to become dark-adapted; if the mushroom does not glow, wrap it in waxed paper, wait several hours, and try again. Incautious mushroom hunters have mistaken *Omphalotus olearius* for the Honey Mushroom, *Armillaria mellea,* and the edible Chanterelles. Eating the Jack-o'-Lantern brings on severe gastric upset lasting for hours or days.

Omphalotus olearius, the Jack-o'-Lantern

Omphalotus olearius

Lentinus lepideus, the Scaly Mushroom or Train Wrecker (Edible). Late spring to fall. Cap 2 to 4 inches across, white or pale brown with brownish spotlike scales; stem 1 to 3 inches long, white, solid, sometimes with scales. Gill edges resemble saw-teeth. Odor like anise or licorice. Spore print white to pale yellowish. Usually occurs singly or in groups of two to four, on wood of conifers and hardwood trees, logs, posts, stumps, even creosoted railroad ties. Its fragrance and toothed gill edges distinguish this mushroom. Except when very young, *Lentinus lepideus* is so tough that it is generally used in making soup or as an addition to gravies; the woody stem is discarded.

Oudemansiella radicata *(Xerula furfuracea, Collybia radicata),* the Rooted Oudemansiella (Edible). Summer and fall. Cap 1 to 4 inches across, grayish brown to smoky brown; flesh white, generally

Lentinus lepideus,
the Scaly Mushroom

Lentinus lepideus

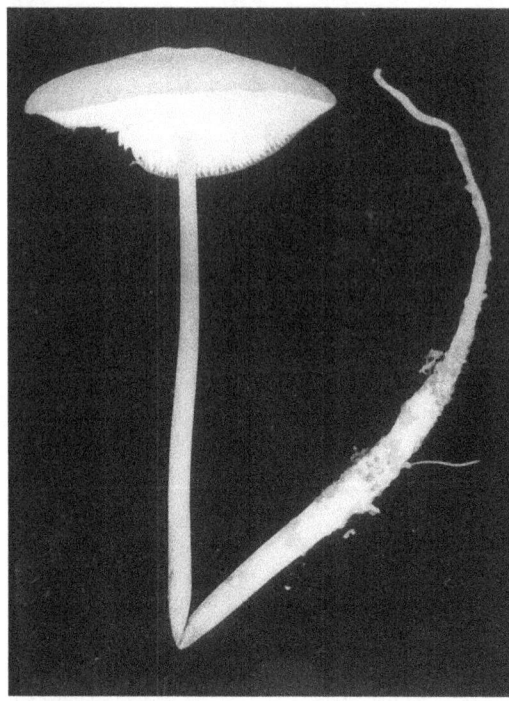

Oudemansiella radicata, the Rooted Oudemansiella

wrinkled or roughened radiately; stem 2 to 8 inches long, slender, brittle, ending below in a long rootlike extension that penetrates an additional 8 to 10 inches into the ground, usually obliquely. Spore print white. A tall, slender, graceful mushroom, *Oudemansiella radicata* occurs as a few scattered specimens or in larger groups in open woods, on stumps and buried tree roots. Careful digging will unearth the rootlike base.

Flammulina velutipes *(Collybia velutipes),* the Velvet Stalk or Winter Mushroom (Edible). Early spring to late fall, sometimes winter. Cap reddish yellow or tawny, very slimy, 1 to 3 inches across, convex but soon flat, smooth; stem 1 to 4 inches long and less than ¼ inch thick, stuffed or hollow, brown or tawny-brown, sometimes almost black, covered with dense, velvety brown to blackish hairs when mature. Spore print white. Usually occurs in dense clusters on dead standing trees, old stumps, logs, and decaying wood, particularly elm, poplar, aspen, and willow. This mushroom is easily distinguished by its dark hairy stem and slimy cap; in cold weather, the slime becomes a thick glutinous coating. The caps should be peeled before cooking to rid them of clinging dirt, leaves, and other debris. The cold-hardy Velvet Stalk sometimes emerges during winter thaws, especially on south-facing slopes.

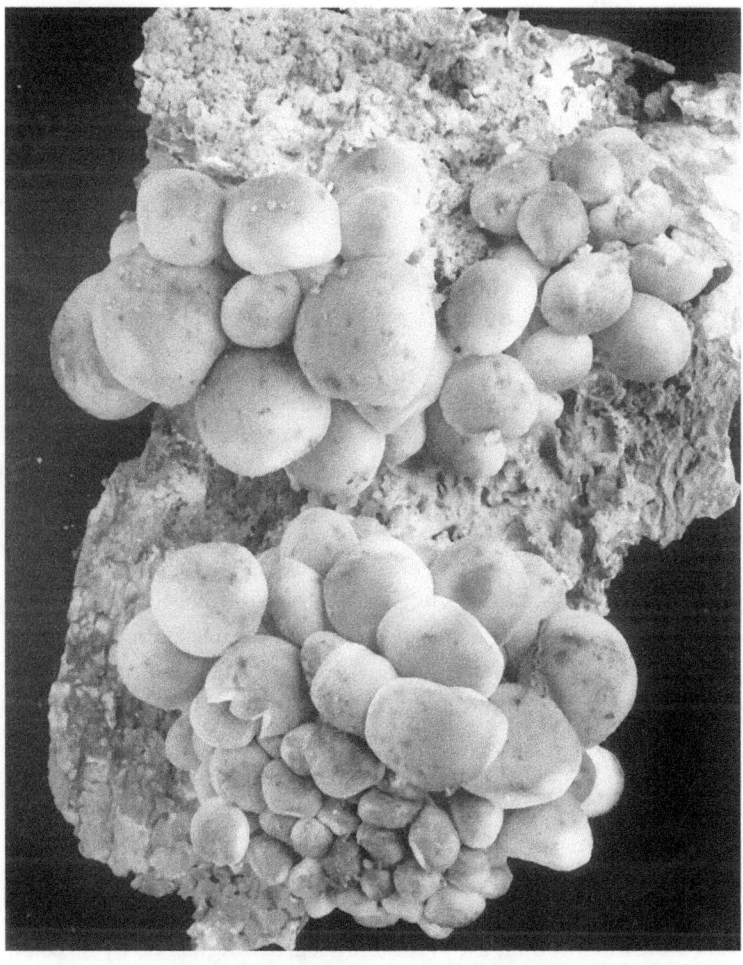

Flammulina velutipes, the Velvet Stalk

Flammulina velutipes

Lepista nuda (*Clitocybe nuda, Tricholoma nudum,* and *Tricholoma personatum*), the Wood Blewit (Edible). Late summer to fall. Cap 2 to 6 inches across, convex, expanded, slightly depressed or flat, thick, smooth, pale gray when young, pale lavender or purple when mature; margin at first downy or fuzzy and turned inward; flesh lavender or whitish, appearing water-soaked in wet weather; stem 1 to 3 inches long and ½ to 1 inch thick, solid, white or colored like the cap, swollen into a bulb at the base. Spore print pale pink or pinkish tan. Occurs in groups or clusters of many individuals on the ground, in woods and open places, gardens, around compost and sawdust piles, and in heaps of leaves. One of the most delicious of the edible mushrooms, the Wood Blewit is distinguished by its color, pinkish spore print, and autumnal emergence

Lepista nuda, the
Wood Blewitt,
(above and below)

Boletes

The boletes are a group of fleshy fungi with caps and stems. They differ from the gilled mushrooms in that the lower surfaces of their caps bear pores (openings of tubes) rather than gills. Unlike the polypores, which also have pores, the tube layer of a bolete separates cleanly from the cap flesh. Boletes grow on the ground, whereas most polypores grow on wood.

Most of the boletes are edible and are considered very tasty. However, a few can cause illness. Any species with orange or bright red pores is very likely to be poisonous. To be safe, avoid eating any bolete whose cap flesh turns blue after wounding, as when broken or scored with a fingernail, knife blade, or other sharp edge.

Boletus bicolor, the Two-Colored Bolete (Edible). Summer and fall. Cap 2 to 6 inches across, convex, dry, firm, becoming softer and deep rosy red or becoming paler and spotted or stained with yellow; flesh of cap thick, pale or distinctly yellow, deep golden yellow after exposure; stem 1 to 4 inches long, ¼ to ½ inch thick (rarely 1 inch), solid, typically yellow on the top third and red on the lower two-thirds. The stem flesh turns blue when wounded; the tubes, bright yellow or reddish yellow, slowly change to blue when wounded. Spore print olive. Occurs singly and in small groups in woods, especially oak stands, and on lawns in shady places. The similar Brick-Cap Bolete, *Boletus sensibilis,* reportedly causes vomiting, diarrhea, and abdominal pain; it changes color to blue instantly when wounded.

Boletus edulis, the Edible Bolete, King Bolete, or Cèpe (Edible). Summer and fall. Cap 4 to 7 inches across, convex to expanded, smooth, grayish red to brownish red, usually paler on the lobed or

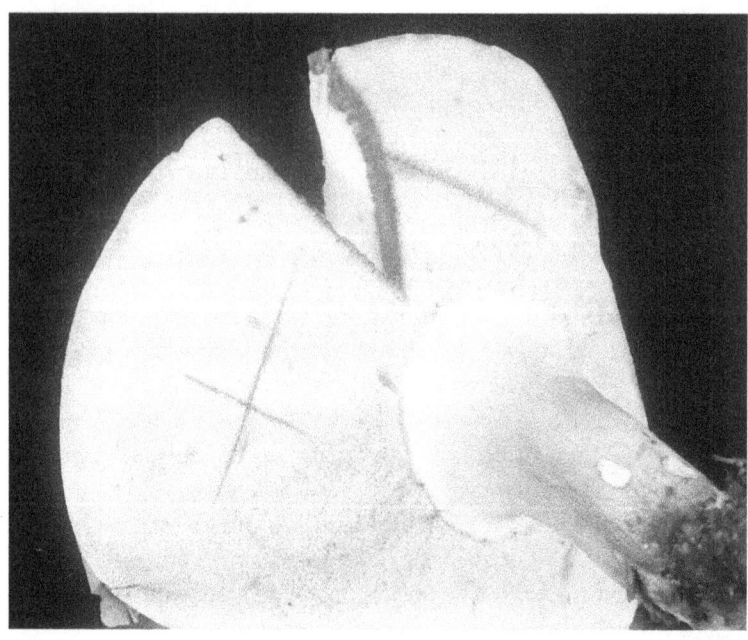

Boletus bicolor, the Two-Colored Bolete (above and below)

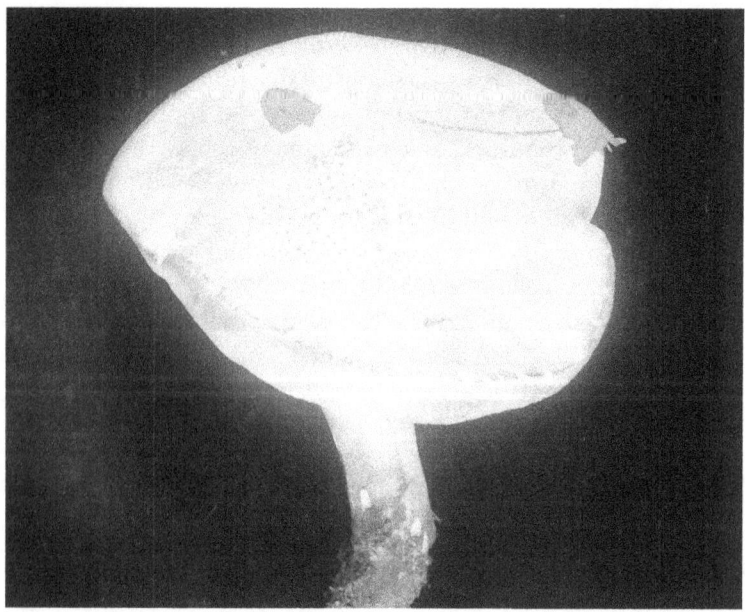

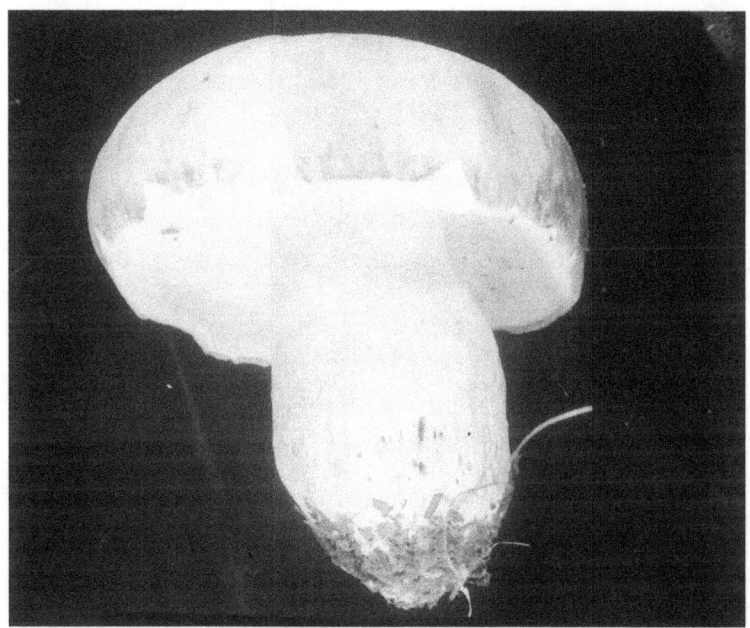

Boletus edulis, the Edible Bolete

slightly overlapping margin, with a moist or slippery surface; flesh of cap thick, white or yellowish, reddish beneath the outer skin layer; stem 2 to 6 inches long and ¼ to 1½ inches thick, sometimes slightly thickened at the base, otherwise equally thick; flesh of stem solid, white, yellowish, or brownish, with a raised network of white lines; tubes at first stuffed, white, then yellow, and finally greenish. Does not stain blue when wounded. Olive-brown spore print. Usually occurs singly or in small groups in coniferous and mixed woods. Found widely throughout North America, *Boletus edulis* is one of the most popular edible mushrooms. The Bitter Bolete, *Tylopilus felleus (Boletus felleus)*, has a very similar appearance but yields a pink to pinkish brown spore print. Although not believed to be poisonous, it has an extremely unpleasant taste.

Leccinum scabrum *(Boletus scaber)*, the Rough-Stemmed Bolete, Scaber Stalk, or Birch Bolete (Edible). Summer and fall, especially after cool, wet spells. Cap 1½ to 5 inches across, convex

Leccinum scabrum,
the Rough-Stemmed
Bolete (above and
below)

to flat, usually smooth but often pitted, roughened, or wrinkled; cap color variable from straw to yellowish brown or dark brown, especially where bruised; tubes whitish when young, then tan and darker brown, sometimes blackish (but not blue) when bruised; stem 2 to 6 inches long, tapering upward, ½ to 1 inch thick, solid, roughened with small brown or black dots or ridges, appearing as though scorched or held in sooty smoke. Olive-buff to brown spore print. Occurs on the ground in woods, particularly beneath birches, and in swamps and open places. This rather variable fungus may represent a complex of several or many different species.

Suillus spraguei *(Suillus pictus, Boletinus pictus),* the Painted Bolete (Edible). Summer and fall. Cap 1 to 5 inches across, convex or nearly flat, dark red when fresh, dry to the touch, hairy and spotted with red scales separated from each other by yellow cracks; cap flesh yellowish, bruising pink or red; stem 1½ to 3 inches long and ¼ to ¾ inch thick, slightly swollen at base, solid; a whitish veil or membrane covers the pore surface of young caps, and remnants

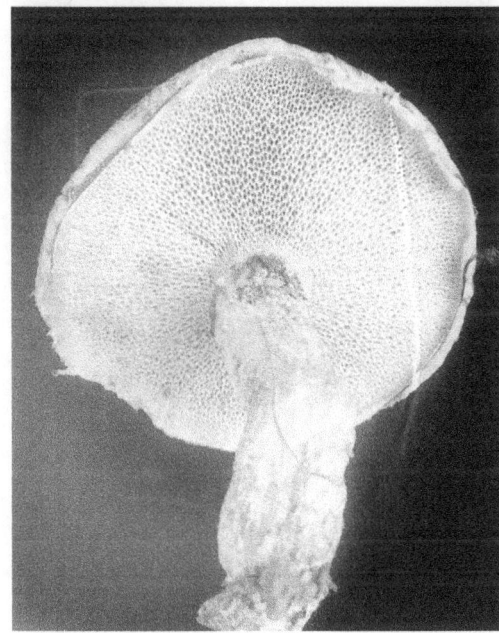

Suillus spraguei,
the Painted Bolete

Suillus spraguei
(above and below)

of the ruptured veil often remain attached to the margin of the cap. Olive-brown spore print. Occurs singly and in groups in woods, often under white pine, and in bogs and wet mossy habitats, where it may fruit even during drought.

Strobilomyces strobilaceus *(Strobilomyces floccopus)*, the Old Man of the Woods (Edible). Summer and fall. Cap 3 to 6 inches across, convex then flat, fleshy, firm, dry, shaggy with numerous coarse black scales and warts, color between scales pale to grayish white, flesh white, changing to red and then black where wounded; a veil or membrane covers the pores when young, and remnants may be seen attached to the margin of mature caps; stem 3 to 5 inches long and ¼ to ½ inch thick, solid, hairy. Spore print black. Usually occurs singly or a few in a scattered group, on the ground or on rotted wood beneath trees. While some experts rate this mushroom a good edible (especially when young), most label it so-so. The Old Man of the Woods does not rot readily and often remains standing, dried out and moldy, far into the fall.

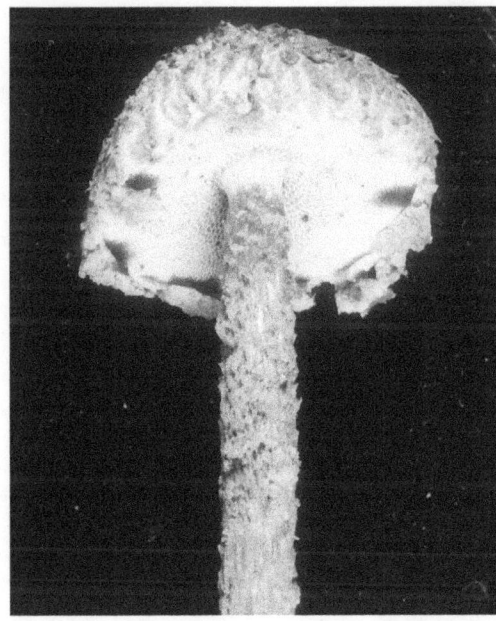

Strobilomyces strobilaceus, the Old Man of the Woods

Polypores

Polypores resemble boletes in that most of them have a layer of tubes, the openings of which are pores visible on their lower surfaces. The tube layer of polypores does not separate cleanly from the rest of the cap, as it does on boletes. Also, most polypores grow on wood while boletes grow on the ground. Most polypores are too tough to be edible; the three species described here are noteworthy exceptions.

Fistulina hepatica, the Beefsteak Mushroom (Edible). Summer and fall. Cap 2 to 8 inches across, ½ to 1 inch thick, slightly convex to flat, tongue-shaped, blood red, soft, and slightly sticky when young; flesh white, streaked with red, soft, with bloodlike juice; stem absent, or if present, short and attached to the side of the cap, ¾ to 4 inches long. Spore print pale rusty brown. Occurs singly or a few in clusters, on stumps and logs or living trees, especially oak and chestnut. Particularly common in the South. The Latin species name means "liver" and refers to the fruiting bodies' shape and color. Some mycophagists praise this mushroom's flavor, while others say it is too sour.

Grifola frondosa *(Polyporus frondosus)*, the Hen of the Woods (Edible). Fruits in fall. The fruiting body is a more or less globose mass of many lobed caps, soft and fleshy at first, then becoming fleshy-tough; individual caps fan- or spoon-shaped, 1 to 3 inches across, grayish, drab, or pale mouse gray; pore surface pure white to yellowish, pores very small; stem compound, branched, short and thick, white. Spore print white. Occurs singly at base of stumps or trunks of oak, elm, and black-gum trees, often appearing in the

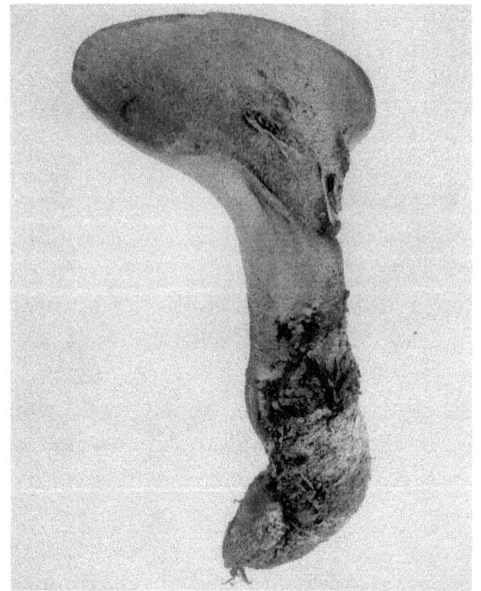

Fistulina hepatica, the
Beefsteak Mushroom

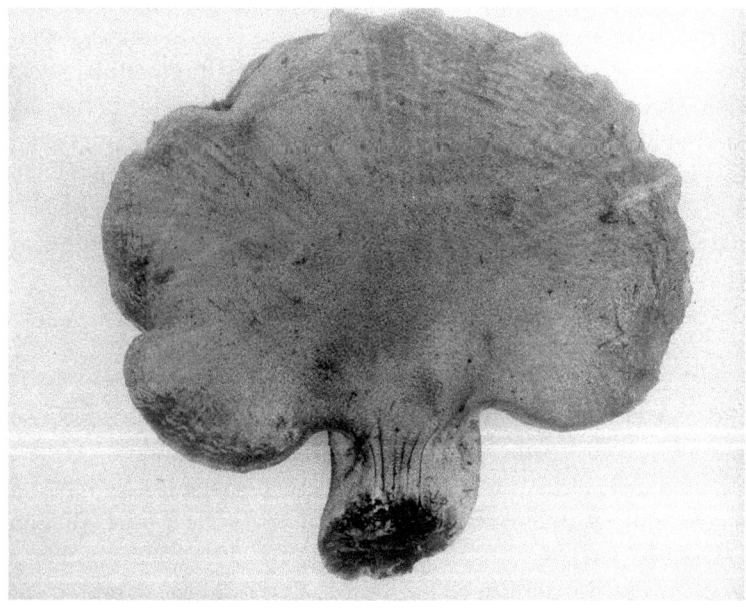

Fistulina hepatica

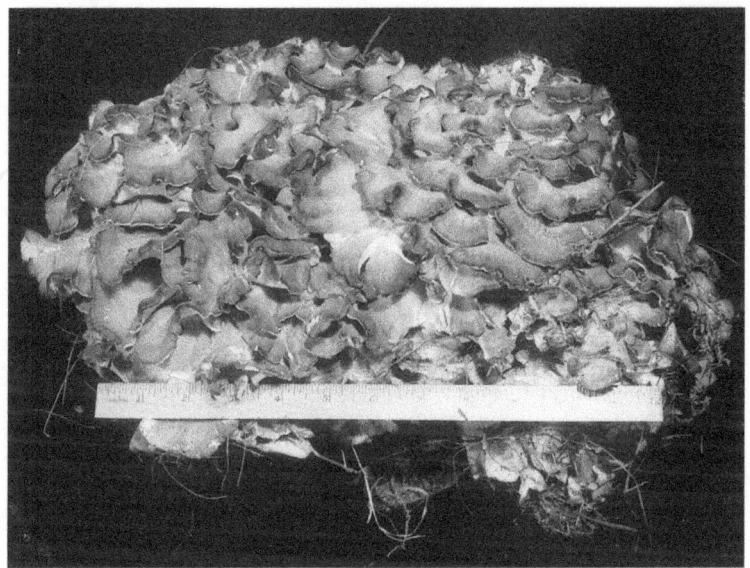

Grifola frondosa, the Hen of the Woods

same spot for several years. The entire fruiting body may be 2 feet across and weigh 10 pounds. This mushroom has an excellent flavor when young but deteriorates fairly quickly.

Laetiporus sulphureus *(Polyporus sulphureus)*, the Sulphur Shelf or Chicken of the Woods (Edible). Late summer and fall. A large, conspicuous mushroom, 8 to 24 inches broad, fleshy and watery to rather firm when fresh, drying to a rigid, brittle consistency; clusters of the shelflike caps may overlap each other, or caps may be clustered together like a bouquet of flowers; upper surface of caps salmon, sulphur yellow, or bright orange, weathering to chalk white as time passes; margin smooth, at first thick and blunt, later thinner; inner tissue white, light yellow, or pale salmon, ¼ to ¾ inch thick; pores very small, tubes ¼ to ½ inch long, pore surface bright sulphur yellow to cream or white. Spore print white. On stumps, trunks, and logs of deciduous and coniferous trees, especially oaks. Its color, shape, and growth on wood make it difficult to confuse this

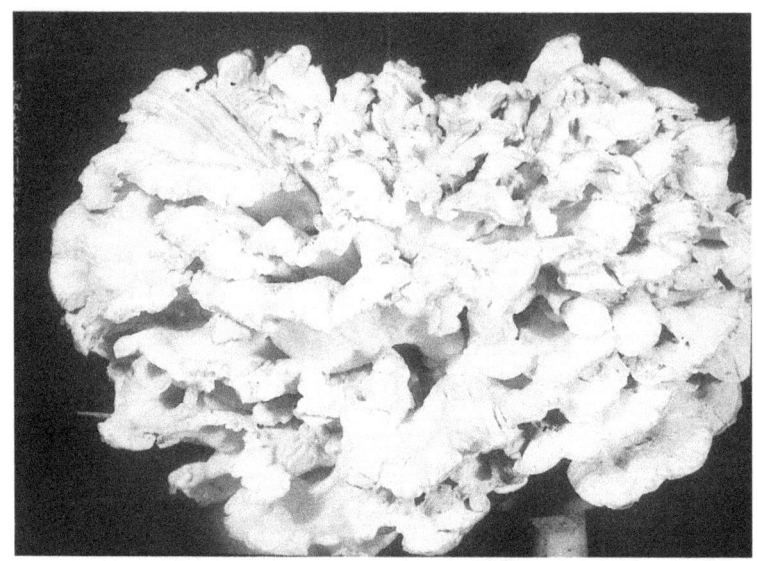

Laetiporus sulphureus, the Sulphur Shelf

Laetiporus sulphureus
in the wild

species with any other. Note where it is collected, for it may appear again in the same year and for several years thereafter. Large fruitings can weigh 20 or more pounds. For eating, select the fresh young fruiting bodies and the tender edges of older ones. In some locales, deer have learned to feed on *Laetiporus sulphureus.*

Toothed Fungi

Hericium coralloides *(Hydnum coralloides)*, the Comb Tooth (Edible). Late summer and fall. Fruiting body tufted, roundish, pure white becoming yellowish with age, 4 to 12 inches across; composed of many branches, which appear lacelike because of numerous delicate teeth that hang downward; teeth up to ¾ inch long. Spore print white. Occurs singly, often on decaying stumps and logs of beech, maple, oak, and other trees. There has been much confusion among mycologists and taxonomists in separating and naming the different *Hericium* species, none of which are poisonous.

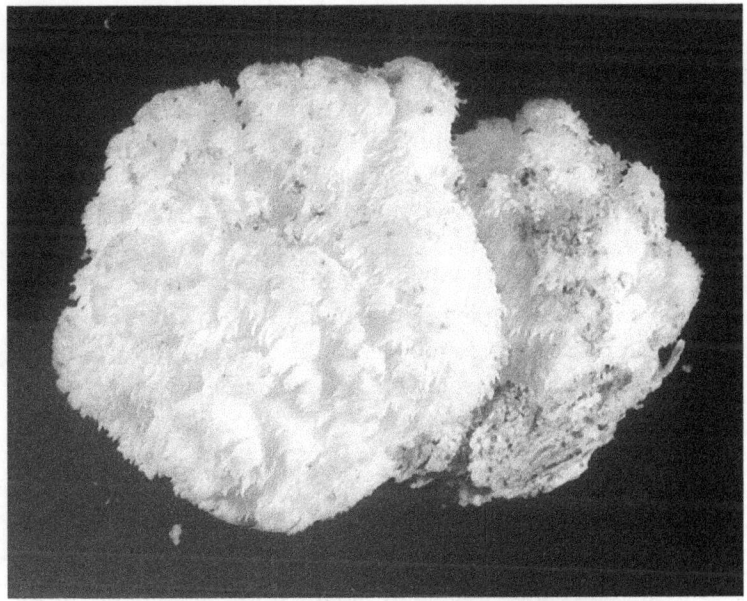

Hericium coralloides, the Comb Tooth

Hericium erinaceus, the Hedgehog Mushroom

Hericium erinaceus, the Hedgehog Mushroom, Bearded Hedgehog, or Bearded Tooth (Edible). Summer and fall. Fleshy, white to creamy white, forming a roundish or pendulous tuft 2 to 10 inches across, narrowing behind to a fairly small point of attachment; teeth hang downward, crowded, slender, tapering, sharp at point, ¾ to 2 inches long. Spore print white. Occurs singly from wounds, crotches, and knotholes of living deciduous trees, most often on oak, rarely on logs and stumps; if it is high up in a tree, a stick can be used to poke it free. This species becomes tough with age and should be eaten only when young. Its shape, sharp-appearing teeth or spines, and growth on wood make the Hedgehog easy to identify.

Hydnum repandum *(Dentinum repandum),* the Spreading Hydnum or Sweet Tooth (Edible). Summer and early fall. Resembles many other mushrooms in having a cap and stem, but the lower surface of the cap is covered with white to cream-colored

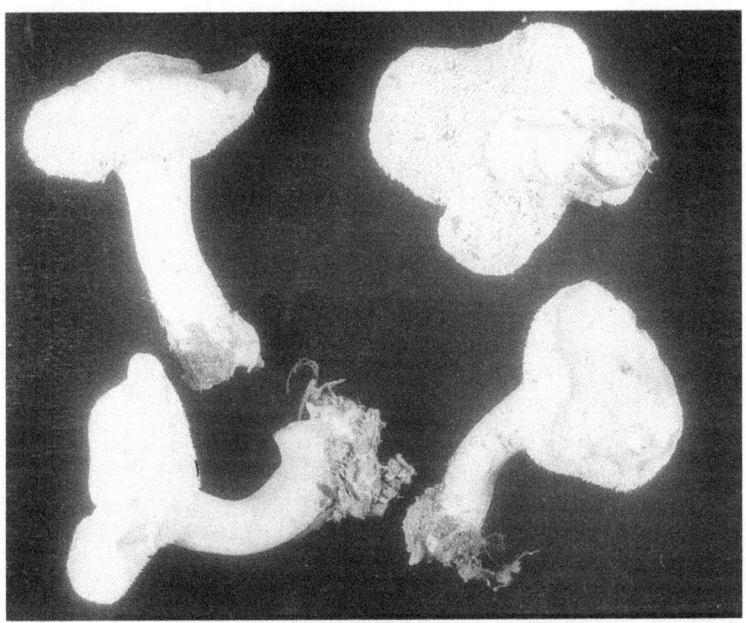

Hydnum repandum, the Spreading Hydnum

teeth, which are straight, smooth, rounded, pointed at the tip, and ⅛ to ⅜ inch long; cap 1 to 5 inches across, pale yellow to pale red and sometimes brown, convex but irregular, smooth, fragile, margin wavy; stem stout, white, solid, 1 to 3 inches long and ½ to ¾ inch thick. White spore print. Occurs singly or in small clusters in woods and open places, on soil or among grass or leaf debris.

Coral Fungi

Clavaria, the Coral Fungi. Their characteristic branching form distinguishes these fungi; the upper parts of the branches produce the spores. Some coral fungi grow on the ground in forested areas, while others grow from wood. Some are bitter to the taste, have a disagreeable odor, or are tough, but many have an excellent flavor. Because of their brittleness, they are sometimes used in soups and gravies. One species in this group, *Ramaria formosa*, has been reported to cause severe poisoning, and others produce gastric upset. The different species are very hard to identify; mycologists often must use microscopic features to separate them. It makes sense not to eat any of the coral fungi.

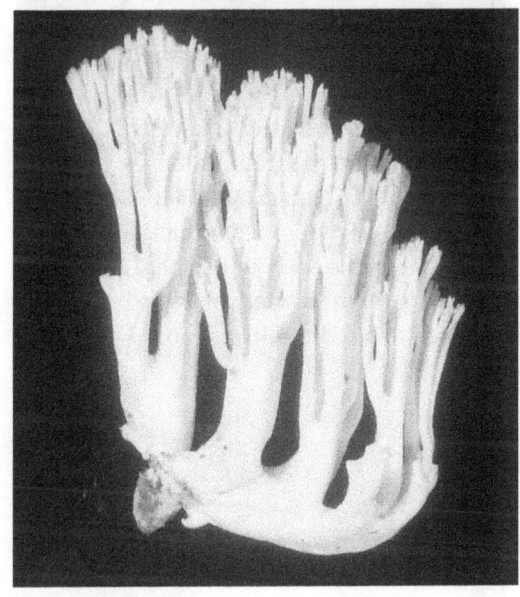

Clavaria species

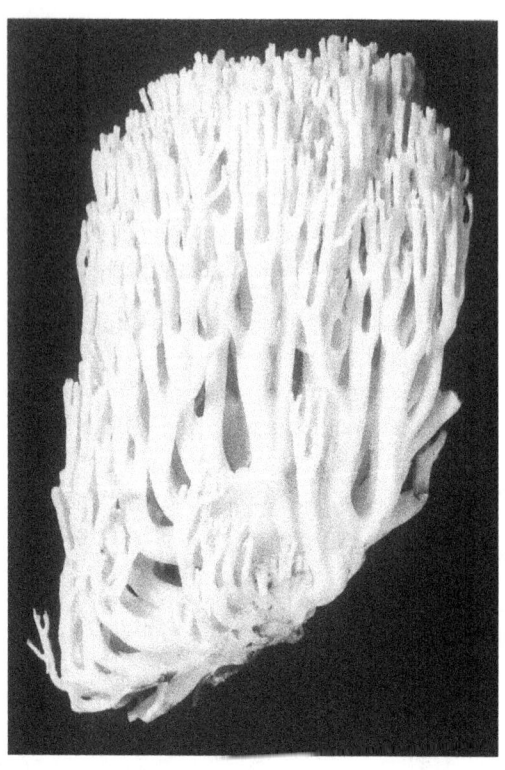

Ramaria botrytis,
the Clustered Coral

Ramaria botrytis *(Clavaria botrytis),* the Clustered Coral or Cauliflower Coral (Edible). Summer and fall. Branches pallid at base, with wine red or pink tips at the branch ends; 4 to 12 inches in diameter. Stalk or base large and fleshy, branches thick and robust, with blunt tips; flesh somewhat brittle and white. Spore color light orange-brown. Fruits on the ground in wooded areas. Although this species is generally considered to be edible, it has caused purgative effects in some people.

Club and
Funnel Fungi

Craterellus cornucopioides, the Horn of Plenty (Edible). Summer and fall. Cap dark gray to blackish brown, thin, flexible, hollow to base, shaped like a trumpet, about 1 to 3 inches across flaring top, 2 to 4 inches long; stem very short, merging with and the same color as the cap; lower or outside surface of cap smooth to slightly wrinkled with primitive foldlike gills. Spore print white. Occurs as fairly large numbers of individuals in scattered clumps, sometimes in tufts, on the ground in deciduous woods, often along woods roads

Craterellus cornucopioides, the Horn of Plenty

Cantharellus lateritius, the Smooth Chanterelle

and paths. Highly prized for its excellent flavor. The Black Trumpet, *Craterellus fallax,* is also a choice edible; it looks very similar to the Horn of Plenty but has a more fragrant odor and produces a pale yellow or pink spore print.

Cantharellus lateritius *(Craterellus cantharellus),* the Smooth Chanterelle (Edible). Summer and fall. Cap yellow to yellow-orange, firm, fleshy, convex at first, often becoming slightly funnel-shaped, smooth, 1 to 4 inches broad, margin quite often rolled inward; stem thicker at top than at base, solid, smooth, yellow, 1 to 3 inches long and ¼ to ½ inch thick. Spore print pale salmon to pinkish yellow. Usually occurs in scattered groups of a few to many individuals in open woods, often beneath oaks. The Smooth Chanterelle resembles the Golden Chanterelle, *Cantharellus cibarius,* but lacks gills on the lower surface of the cap, where the flesh is smooth or very faintly veined. Some mycologists attribute to the Smooth Chanterelle a fruity, apricotlike fragrance.

Sponge and Saddle Fungi

Morchella species, the Morels or Sponge Mushrooms (Edible). Spring. The several species of Morels found in the Northeast are so similar that they will be described here only in a general way. All are edible. Height, 2 to 5 inches; cap bell-shaped, conic, or hemispherical, marked with very prominent ridges and furrows or with prominent ridges connected by cross ridges; cap looks like a sponge; caps vary in color from white to gray to tan. Stem distinct, thick, fleshy, and white, cream-colored, or buff. Cap and stem both hollow.

Morchella esculenta,
the Yellow Morel

Spore color white to creamy white. Usually occurs in woods on the ground. Distribution is erratic: Morels grow under tulip trees, oaks, and hickories in open woods; under dead or dying elms; or far removed from trees. They have been found with regularity in uncultivated grassy apple orchards: the older the orchard, the more likely that Morels will emerge there. At times they grow profusely in rich soil along streambanks where overflows are common. Old fencerows in limestone areas may yield them in abundance. Morels often are produced year after year in the same place, and a wet spring promotes their best development. One should look for them especially at the time that the first petals begin to fall from the apple blossoms. The season lasts three or four weeks.

Soak Morels overnight in salt water to drive out insects and slugs, and cut them lengthwise to check for such creatures before

Morchella esculenta

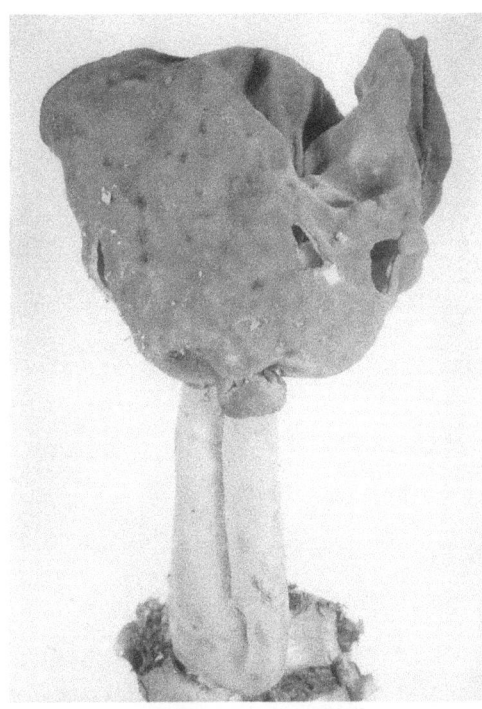

Gyromitra infula,
the False Morel

cooking. The Black Morel (*Morchella elata;* formerly *Morchella angus-ticeps*) has been reported to cause gastrointestinal upset when eaten along with alcohol.

Gyromitra infula *(Helvella infula),* the False Morel (Poisonous). Spring, summer, and fall. Cap 2 to 3 inches broad, irregularly spherical, lobed, sometimes saddle-shaped, bay red to brownish; stem whitish, 2 to 3 inches long, thick, stuffed or hollow. Spore print white. Single, rarely two or three occurring together, in damp places including soil rich with decaying wood. Toxins in False Morels have killed some people who have eaten them. Mycologists disagree on the number of species of False Morels.

Puffballs

The fungi known as puffballs are almost all edible if eaten when young, when the interior flesh is pure white and has a firm consistency. Collectors should cut through the middle of smaller specimens to make sure they are not immature stages of stinkhorn fungi, which have a bad odor, or *Amanita* mushrooms, which can be deadly poisonous. The cut section will show a gelatinous inner layer if the specimen is the early stage of an inedible stinkhorn, or the developing cap and stem if it is an *Amanita*.

Puffballs are so named because the fruiting body is shaped like a ball, and at maturity the powdery spores come puffing out in a dusty cloud when the mushroom is stepped on or squeezed. Puffballs grow on the ground and on rotting wood.

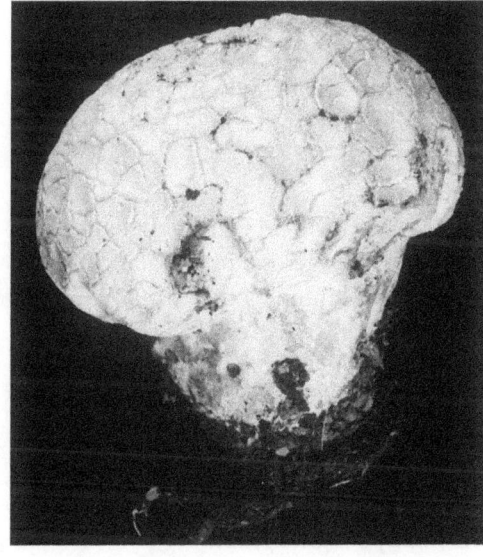

Calvatia craniformis, the Skull-Shaped Puffball

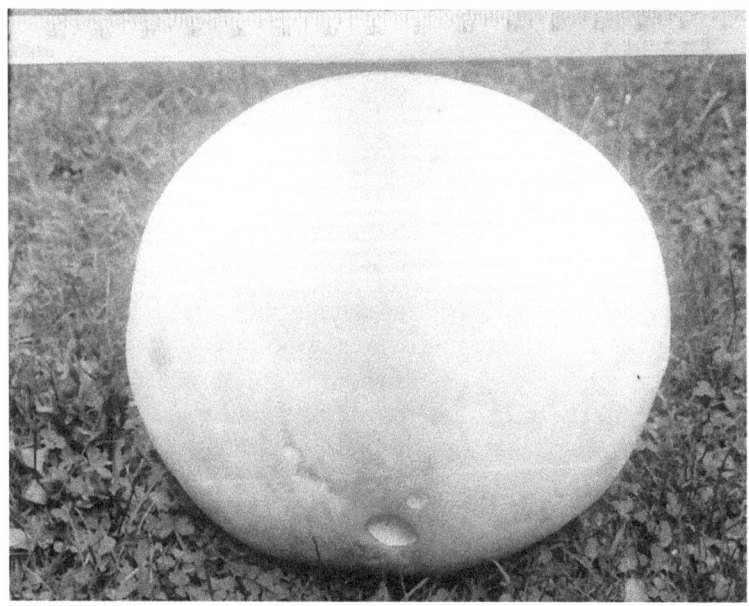

Calvatia gigantea, the Giant Puffball

Calvatia craniformis, the Skull-Shaped Puffball (Edible). Late summer and fall. Round, 3 to 6 inches across, whitish or pinkish brown, smooth, soon cracking into irregular areas, with a short, stemlike base. Mature spore tissue yellow-green. Usually occurs in groups of several to many individuals in grassy meadows and open woods. This species has a fine flavor; it should be peeled and eaten only when young.

Calvatia gigantea, the Giant Puffball (Edible). Summer and fall. Round or egg-shaped, 8 to 24 inches across; practically no stem, attached to the ground by cordlike strands; outer surface smooth although sometimes slightly roughened, like chamois to the touch, white or whitish, later becoming yellow or brown; inner substance pure white at first, changing to yellowish, and finally becoming dingy olive. Occurs singly or in groups of a few, on lawns, in pastures, meadows, and open woods, sometimes on streambanks. This mushroom is so large and has such a unique form that it cannot be mistaken for any other. It is highly sought as food.

Destroying Angel

The mushroom was white. It stood almost to my eight-year-old knees. A shaft of sunlight penetrating the summer woods lit its cap, the ring of tissue around its stem, and the cup surrounding the stem's base. We were collecting, my father and I. We had found Chanterelles and Coral Fungi and Boletes and many other mushrooms, but none so impressive as this white sentinel.

My father was behind me on the trail, so I dug up the mushroom and hurried back. When I gave it to him, he took one look at it and ordered me to wash my hands in a nearby stream. After I obeyed, he explained: I had picked a mushroom so poisonous that particles of it, stuck to my fingers and accidentally swallowed, could have made me deathly ill, and a piece the size of my thumb could have killed me.

He spoke the mushroom's name: Destroying Angel. Years later, when I grew interested in mushrooms again, the Destroying Angel was the first one I studied.

The Destroying Angel is *Amanita virosa*. It belongs to a large and widespread group of fungi, the amanitas, which have been affecting humans for millennia as food, religious symbols, hallucinogens, and poisons. No one really knows how many species of amanitas exist. A respected mycologist recognizes seventy-five worldwide, while the U.S. Department of Agriculture lists over six hundred species, subspecies, and varieties reported from places as various as Perth, Australia, and Blowing Rock, North Carolina.

Amanitas are large, showy mushrooms. Many measure 4 or 5 inches across the cap, and they come in a rainbow of colors—red, orange, brown, yellow, gray, green, white. Although only some of the amanitas are toxic, the group as a whole causes more than 90 percent of all fatal mushroom poisonings. The Destroying Angel is the most frequent killer in North America; in Europe, the major culprit is the Death Cap, *Amanita phalloides*. In the latter part of the twentieth century, the Death Cap immigrated to America, probably clinging to the roots of ornamental shrubs. Collectors have found this greenish-capped mushroom in Pennsylvania, Virginia, Delaware, New York, New Jersey, California, Oregon, and Washington.

Unfortunately, many mushroom eaters—or "mycophagists," as they're sometimes called—take to the woods with barely skimmed field guides, blissfully ignorant of Death Caps and Destroying Angels. They look for the mushrooms their grandparents ate in the old country, or they rely on folklore to determine edibility. One bit of folly says a poisonous mushroom, or toadstool, will tarnish a silver spoon. Another declares a mushroom edible if the skin of its cap peels easily. A third says poisonous mushrooms never grow on rotting wood. A fourth holds that rice cooked with a toxic mushroom will turn red. All of these beliefs are false, and each year people who rely on them are poisoned. Even field guides give no complete answer: a mushroom's appearance often changes as it matures, and basing an identification on a single photograph can be a costly mistake.

It is not known how many people die from mushroom poisoning each year, but probably scores in America and hundreds in Europe. One of the most tragic incidents occurred in Poland in 1918, when thirty-one children died after eating a mushroom dish at school. In 1975, a Swiss newspaper reported fifty-four local deaths from mushroom poisoning during a short period in late summer. In California and the Pacific Northwest, many Asian refugees have perished after mistaking amanitas for common edible mushrooms in their native lands.

As part of a general move back to nature, increasing numbers of Americans are eating wild mushrooms, and many are poisoning themselves in the process. Foragers confuse Destroying Angels with Meadow Mushrooms, the group that gives us our common grocery-store variety. Or young amanitas, called buttons, are picked along with puffballs, which they somewhat resemble. (When preparing puffballs, the wise mycophagist slices his specimens vertically: an amanita or other gilled mushroom is revealed by a miniature but perfectly formed stalk and cap.)

An amanita has two distinguishing characteristics. The first is a cuplike structure, called a volva, at the base of the stem. The mushroom looks like it is growing out of this cup. The second characteristic is a white spore print, a pattern laid down by millions of microscopic spores—reproductive cells that can be thought of as tiny seeds—falling from the gills on the underside of the mushroom's cap. To make a spore print, separate the cap from the stem,

Three stages of *Amanita virosa*

place the cap gills-down on a piece of black paper, and wait a couple of hours. If the mushroom is an amanita, a white-on-black negative image of the gills will appear. Other mushrooms may make yellow, pink, brown, purple-brown, or black spore prints. (Note that a number of mushrooms yielding colored spore prints also are poisonous.) A few non-amanitas have volvas, and some make white spore prints, but only an amanita exhibits both. Another trait of most, though not all, amanitas is a ring of tissue on the stem, a remainder of the partial veil that enclosed the growing mushroom.

Amanita toxins, called amanitins, are especially potent. A single bite of mushroom can bring on an agonizing, lingering death. The stem, gills, and cap are equally deadly. The toxins survive cooking, freezing, drying. And while most poisonous mushrooms cause symptoms an hour or two after they're eaten, an amanita doesn't tip its hand for six to twenty-four hours. A victim may enjoy another meal, perhaps finishing his collection of wild mushrooms, go to work, even sleep while the poison invades his body.

Finally, he is seized by stomach pains, violent vomiting, and diarrhea. But purging the system does no good, because the mushrooms have already been digested. If the victim is not hospitalized, and if he ate more than one average-size mushroom cap, the illness worsens and usually causes death.

In a hospital, doctors can relieve the vomiting and diarrhea and correct the dangerous dehydration they produce. The patient feels better and seems to recover. He may even be discharged if his illness has not been diagnosed. Then, three to six days later, the symptoms reappear. In many cases, the victim dies. An autopsy reveals massive liver and kidney damage.

Recently, scientists have traced the poison's path. The first symptoms—nausea, vomiting, and diarrhea—commence after the toxin enters the bloodstream through lesions it causes in the stomach and intestines. Later, while the victim seems to be getting better, the poison is traveling to the liver. During the second bout of illness, the poison kills individual liver cells. If the patient hangs on, his blood takes the toxin to the kidneys. The kidneys try to excrete the poison with the urine, but it attacks and injures the convoluted tubules, reentering the blood. It returns to the liver to do more damage. And again to the kidneys, the blood, the liver.

In the past, some doctors fed their patients a sugared hash of the stomachs of three rabbits and the brains of seven, based on an incorrect belief that rabbits are immune to amanitins. Today a chemical called thioctic acid seems to be saving lives, but it is still considered experimental. Another technique involves pumping out the stomach bile, the medium through which the toxins move from the liver and back into the bloodstream after kidney function has been impaired. Survivors sometimes require liver transplants.

But not all amanitas are poisonous. After learning about the group, I decided to try one of the safe species to compare its flavor with those of the Morel, the Shaggy Mane, the Sulphur Shelf, and other edible mushrooms I have learned to identify and prepare.

I settled on the Grisette, *Amanita vaginata*, widely eaten in Europe, where it also occurs. Grisette means gray, which is the color of these mushrooms. They lack a ring on the stem, a feature that helps in identifying them. I found and picked two dozen Grisettes on the edge of a golf course. I took them to my father, a mycology professor for thirty years, and he verified my identification. I cooked the Grisettes in butter and served them over toast.

I think my stomach was jumpy even before I lifted a fork. There are no records of poisoning by the Grisette, and I knew rationally that I was not eating toxic mushrooms, but I had read too many accounts of slow, cruel deaths. I never finished my meal, and for two days after I found myself checking for the dreaded delayed pains. I have not eaten any amanitas since.

The most prolific mushroom eaters are wildlife, and even they seem to steer clear of most amanitas. Dr. Orson K. Miller, in *Mushrooms of North America,* writes that he has never found rodent tooth marks on a white amanita. "The rodents have apparently learned their lessons well," Miller says. "They may shy away from the chlorinelike odor which is often very faint to strong."

Miller's observation points to a possible reason why the Destroying Angel and the Death Cap evolved their toxins: to guard against being eaten, improving their chances of maturing and releasing spores. Many species of plants and animals protect themselves with bad-tasting metabolic products, but why an organism should develop such an unobtrusive, slow, and deadly poison remains a mystery. Also, toxic power can vary from mushroom to mushroom: one Destroying Angel may have little or no poison, and another a hundred yards down the path may be loaded.

Often we assume that everything in nature—every property, structure, and behavior—must have evolved in response to an environmental pressure. Perhaps an amanita's poisons confer no advantages to the fungus, and it is only plain bad luck that they kill.

INDEX OF EDIBLE AND POISONOUS MUSHROOMS BY MONTH OF FIRST APPEARANCE OF FRUITING BODIES IN CENTRAL PENNSYLVANIA

The fruiting bodies of some fungi come up only during brief periods; others may be found over a wide span of months. The following chart reflects average dates for mushroom emergence in central Pennsylvania. Areas to the north will generally have later dates for the same species, and areas to the south will show earlier dates. Weather, including abnormal temperatures and rainfall, can also influence the date of appearance of mushrooms.

Also see information in the text regarding the emergence of the different mushroom species.

MARCH AND APRIL
Fungi with Gills
Flammulina velutipes, the Velvet Stalk or Winter Mushroom (Edible)
Coprinus micaceus, the Mica Cap or Glistening Coprinus (Edible)

MAY AND EARLY JUNE
Fungi with Gills
Amanita muscaria, the Fly Amanita or Fly Agaric (Poisonous)
Amanita species (Poisonous)
Oudemansiella radicata, the Rooted Oudemansiella (Edible)
Coprinus atramentarius, the Inky Cap or Tippler's Bane (Edible)
Coprinus comatus, the Shaggy Mane (Edible)
Lentinus lepideus, the Scaly Mushroom or Train Wrecker (Edible)

Fungi without Gills
Morchella species, the Morels or Sponge Mushrooms (Edible)
Gyromitra infula, the False Morel (Poisonous)

JUNE
Fungi with Gills
Psathyrella candolleana (Edible)
Panaeolus retirugis (Poisonous)
Pleurotus ostreatus, the Oyster Mushroom (Edible)

JULY AND AUGUST

Fungi with Gills

Agaricus campestris, the Meadow Mushroom or Field Mushroom (Edible)

Amanita bisporigera (Poisonous)

Amanita cothurnata (Poisonous)

Armillaria mellea, the Honey Mushroom or Oak Fungus (Edible)

Cantharellus cibarius, the Golden Chanterelle (Edible)

Omphalotus olearius, the Jack-o'-Lantern or False Chanterelle (Poisonous)

Macrolepiota procera, the Parasol Mushroom (Edible)

Chlorophyllum molybdites (Poisonous)

Fungi without Gills

Pore Fungi

Boletus bicolor, the Two-Colored Bolete (Edible)

Boletus edulis, the Edible Bolete, King Bolete, or Cèpe (Edible)

Leccinum scabrum, the Rough-Stemmed Bolete, Scaber Stalk, or Birch Bolete (Edible)

Suillus spraguei, the Painted Bolete (Edible)

Strobilomyces strobilaceus, the Old Man of the Woods (Edible)

Fistulina hepatica, the Beefsteak Mushroom (Edible)

Laetiporus sulphureus, the Sulphur Shelf or Chicken of the Woods (Edible)

Coral Fungi

Clavaria, the Coral Fungi (both Edible and Poisonous species)

Ramaria botrytis, the Clustered Coral or Cauliflower Coral (Edible)

Toothed Fungi

Hericium erinaceus, the Hedgehog Mushroom, Bearded Hedgehog, or Bearded Tooth (Edible)

Club and Funnel Fungi

Cantharellus lateritius, the Smooth Chanterelle (Edible)

Craterellus cornucopioides, the Horn of Plenty (Edible)

AUGUST AND SEPTEMBER

Fungi with Gills

Amanita cokeri (Poisonous)

Amanita virosa, the Destroying Angel (Poisonous)

Lactarius deliciosus, the Delicious Lactarius or Orange-Latex Milky (Edible)

Lactarius indigo, the Blue Lactarius or Indigo Milky (Edible)

Hypsizygus tessulatus, the Elm Pleurotus (Edible)

Fungi without Gills

Pore Fungi

Grifola frondosa, the Hen of the Woods (Edible)

Toothed Fungi

Hericium coralloides, the Comb Tooth (Edible)

Hydnum repandum, the Spreading Hydnum or Sweet Tooth (Edible)

Puffballs

Calvatia craniformis, the Skull-Shaped Puffball (Edible)

Calvatia gigantea, the Giant Puffball (Edible)

OCTOBER AND NOVEMBER

Fungi with Gills

Hypholoma sublateritium, the Brick Cap or Brick Top (Edible)

Lepista nuda, the Wood Blewit (Edible)

References

Barron, George. *Mushrooms of Northeast North America*. Edmonton, Alberta: Lone Pine, 1999. *A thorough field guide with up-to-date taxonomic names. Scientific information about fungi is presented along with color photographs and species accounts.*

Bessette, Alan, and Walter Sundberg. *Mushrooms: A Quick Reference Guide to Mushrooms of North America*. New York: Macmillan, 1987. *A basic field guide with color photographs.*

Fergus, Charles. *Natural Pennsylvania: Exploring the State Forest Natural Areas*. Mechanicsburg, PA: Stackpole Books, 2002. *Pennsylvanians can find many fungi in the state-managed natural areas, particularly ones that preserve stands of old-growth forest.*

Fischer, David W., and Alan Bessette. *Edible Wild Mushrooms of North America: A Field-to-Kitchen Guide*. Austin, TX: University of Texas Press, 1992. *Covers over one hundred edible mushrooms and gives gourmet recipes.*

Lincof, Gary. *The Audubon Society Field Guide to North American Mushrooms*. New York: Alfred A. Knopf, 1981. *A good compact field guide.*

McKnight, Kent H., and Vera McKnight. *A Field Guide to Mushrooms*. Boston: Houghton Mifflin, 1987. *In the Peterson Field Guide Series, with watercolor illustrations.*

Miller, Orson K., Jr. *Mushrooms of North America*. New York: Dutton, 1979. *An extensive manual with detailed keys to the different groups of fungi, along with color photographs; available in both a hardback version and a smaller field-guide format.*

Phillips, Roger. *Mushrooms of North America.* New York: Little, Brown, 1991. *Short descriptive passages accompany over one thousand color photographs of specimens made in studio settings. The book is in a large format and makes an excellent desk reference to be used in combination with the smaller field guides.*

Schaechter, Elio. *In the Company of Mushrooms: A Biologist's Tale.* Cambridge, MA: Harvard University Press, 1997. *A passionate, informed account of the biology and history of fungi, written by a scientist.*

Acknowledgments

I thank the following people for the help they have given me on this project: Bill Russell, Robert Proctor, Lee Schisler, Herb Cole, Eva Pell, Ginny Imboden, Ronald Pursell, C. B. Wolfe, Elizabeth Brantley, Jim McClure, and Nancy Marie Brown.

Gary Emberger, Ph.D., chair of the Department of Natural Sciences at Messiah College, reviewed the manuscript and made many helpful suggestions, particularly with the identification key.

Special thanks go to Mark Allison of Stackpole Books, with whom I have now worked on five books. An exemplary editor, he has also become a good friend.

I would like to dedicate this book to the memory of my parents, Leonard Fergus and Ruth Foote Fergus.

—Charles Fergus

About the Authors

C. Leonard Fergus, Ph.D., was on the faculty of Pennsylvania State University from 1948 to 1983, when he retired as professor emeritus of botany. He taught general biology, botany, forest pathology, mycology, and other courses, and was curator of the university's mycological herbarium. He died in 1983.

Charles Fergus is the author of twelve books, including the novel *Shadow Catcher*. Three of his most recent titles, all published by Stackpole Books, are *Wildlife of Pennsylvania and the Northeast, Natural Pennsylvania: Exploring the State Forest Natural Areas,* and *Trees of Pennsylvania and the Northeast.*

C. Leonard Fergus (at right) and naturalist and artist Ned Smith examine a nice Sulphur Shelf specimen.

www.ingramcontent.com/pod-product-compliance
Lightning Source LLC
Chambersburg PA
CBHW051452150525
26725CB00016B/216